# MARK IV
## VS
# A7V

## Villers-Bretonneux 1918

First published in Great Britain in 2012 by Osprey Publishing, Midland House, West Way, Botley, Oxford, OX2 0PH, UK 43-01 21st Street, Suite 220B, Long Island City, NY 11101, USA

E-mail: info@ospreypublishing.com

Osprey Publishing is part of the Osprey Group

A CIP catalogue record for this book is available from the British Library

Print ISBN: 978 1 78096 005 0
PDF ebook ISBN: 978 1 78096 007 4
ePub ebook ISBN: 978 1 78096 006 7

Index by Alan Thatcher
Typeset in ITC Conduit and Adobe Garamond
Maps by bounford.com
Originated by PDQ Media, Bungay, UK
Printed in China through Bookbuilders

12 13 14 15 16     10 9 8 7 6 5 4 3 2 1

Osprey Publishing is supporting the Woodland Trust, the UK's leading woodland conservation charity, by funding the dedication of trees.

www.ospreypublishing.com

**Key to military symbols**

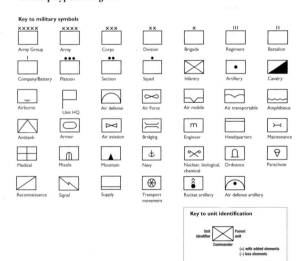

### Acknowledgements

I would like to thank the following individuals for their kind support, without which this book and my other military history endeavours might not have been possible. David Fletcher, historian (The Tank Museum, Bovington); Rainer Strasheim; Steven Zaloga; Joseph Miranda, editor-in-chief, *Modern War*; Colonel (ret) Jerry D. Morelock, PhD, editor-in-chief, *Armchair General*; Claude Balmefrezol; Stephen Pope; Shane Black; Jeff Olshan; Shane Weier; Jean-Marie Brams; Ilias Tsiphlidis; Agnieszka Modrzejewska (Castle Museum, Pless); Nick Reynolds, commissioning editor (Osprey Publishing); the very helpful staff at the NARA microfilm, map, and photograph departments; Mark Whitmore, Director of Collections (Imperial War Museum, London); and my wife, Diana.

### Dedication

To my mom, Carin

### Author's note

Armies, corps and divisions are written as, e.g., Fourth Army (spelled out), III Corps (Roman numerals), and 4th Guards Infantry Division (ordinal). German designations are equivalent and partially anglicized to preserve flavour, e.g., Sturm-Panzerkraftwagen-Abteilung (Stuka) is rendered as Assault Tank Detachment (ATD). Except in certain cases formation names are spelled out to lessen confusion. Any errors or omissions in this work were certainly unintended, and for them I alone bear responsibility.

### Editor's note

For ease of comparison please refer to the following conversion table:

1.6km = 1 mile
0.9m = 1yd
0.3m = 1ft
2.54cm/25.4mm = 1in
4.5 litres = 1 gallon (imperial)
0.45kg = 1lb

### Artist's note

Readers may care to note that the original painting from which the battlescene in this book was prepared is available for private sale. All reproduction copyright whatsoever is retained by the Publishers. All inquiries should be addressed to:

Peter Dennis, 'Fieldhead', The Park, Mansfield, Nottinghamshire NG18 2AT, UK, or email magie.h@ntlworld.com

The Publishers regret that they can enter into no correspondence upon this matter.

# CONTENTS

# INTRODUCTION

At the turn of the 21st century main battle tanks possess a range of internal and external systems designed to project power and protect their crews from a host of threats, including kinetic penetrators, shaped-charge projectiles, intelligent homing submunitions, mines and laser-guided artillery. In addition to active defence munitions and explosive reactive armour, over-pressurized, clean-air conditioned cabins, and multi-layer tungsten, steel, plastic and ceramic armour plates (Chobham) further provide a nuclear, biological and chemical-resistant working environment backed by automatic Halon fire extinguishers, and ammunition- and fuel-separating armoured bulkheads. Operationally, 120mm-plus main guns can launch 1,750m/s projectiles to attack targets over 4,000m away, while 1,500hp engines enable 60-tonne-plus vehicles to achieve speeds of over 70km/h. When integrated within a modern, all-arms fighting force comprising fixed- and rotary-wing aircraft, artillery, and mechanized infantry, the tank represents the core component of any military's conventional, as well as asymmetrical, ground force because of its ability to facilitate the taking and holding of terrain.

A century before, such technologies would have exceeded the wildest imaginings of even the most far-sighted military futurist. While the Industrial Revolution stimulated a host of advances in technology, agriculture, manufacturing and transport during the 18th and 19th centuries, its science-based perspective expanded into chemical, electrical, steel and railway applications. Building on steam-powered motors, German inventors in the late 19th century improved upon the recently developed petrol-powered internal combustion engine, which due to its small size and efficient output, was soon mated to increasingly robust wheeled car, lorry and agricultural tractor designs. Competition and mass production subsequently promoted the rapid maturation and distribution of such technologies in civilian, as well as military applications.

At the outbreak of World War I on 28 July 1914, fielding and maintaining massive armies was no longer the dominant contributor to wartime success that it had been, as technology and manufacturing grew in importance. As had occurred during earlier conflicts, such as the American Civil War and the Franco-Prussian War, railways proved a considerable operational asset in that they transported large numbers of men and materiel literally to the front lines. Road networks similarly retained their battlefield importance, and cars, lorries and motorcycles were correspondingly produced in ever greater numbers. While this would seemingly have helped maintain movement in what many assumed would be a short war, the widespread use of barbed wire, rapid-firing artillery and the machine gun led to an operational stalemate across north-eastern France and Belgium. As defence now proved markedly superior to offence, even the largest armies lacked the ability to penetrate their adversary's interlocked succession of fortified positions, which extended from the English Channel to the Swiss border. With no discernable flank to turn, frontal assaults predominated, which – even if successful – amounted to little more than a tactical breach, as the mass of foot-slogging infantry suffered unsustainable casualties, and lacked the endurance to exploit any opportunities generated. After a year of minimal progress for considerable effort, both sides looked for ways to return manoeuvring to the static Western Front.

Although Germany's offensive to take Paris as the war opened was foiled at the River Marne, the Germans' possession of much of north-eastern France meant the Allies' operational focus was largely based on driving their enemy out. Throughout 1915, the near-pathological French desire to regain lost territory resulted in costly battles at Neuve Chapelle, Second Ypres, Festubert and Loos, especially against a German army that was largely content to incorporate a force-multiplying defensive stance to conserve limited resources. The Germans, having experienced largely fluid battles in the East, decided on a solution to break the stalemate on the Western Front that focused on numerous, heavily armed, specialist infantry assault units, which would infiltrate, isolate and weaken enemy positions prior to the arrival of the masses of their more conventional comrades. While the Allies increasingly adopted such tactics after 1917, their greater resources permitted a broader approach. This ranged from operationally flanking their German and Austro-Hungarian adversaries, for example at Gallipoli and in Italy, to technological and manufacturing solutions, including bullet-resistant 'land battleships'.

A pair of Mark IV (females) during the fighting around Cambrai in 1917. Their front and sponson Lewis machine guns have been removed to avoid getting snagged and damaged in the rugged environment. Note the spotter on the top of each vehicle helping the driver navigate. (*Illustrated War News*)

# CHRONOLOGY

## 1915

**20 February**  Winston Churchill, First Lord of the Admiralty, establishes a 'Landships Committee' to explore domestic tank development.

## 1916

**12 January**  'Centipede', British Mark I's trapezoid-shaped tank prototype, first runs.

**15 September**  Tanks (Mark Is) first used in combat near Delville Wood during the battle of Flers-Courcelette.

**13 November**  Germany initiates development of its first tank, the A7V.

In the early summer of 1918 ATD 2 participated in a demonstration some 40km east of Villers-Bretonneux, while A7Vs 502/540, 505 and 507 underwent transition to *Sockellafette* mounts at the nearby workshop. The closest vehicle is likely to be 503 (with removed front/ rear conn plates), with 505 or 507 in the middle (before the change) and 504 in the distance. (NARA)

ATD 2's 'Wotan' (563) entraining on 5 June 1918, north-east of Reims, on a 4-axle 32-tonne SSml flat-car (subsequently damaged by the tank's weight), from a makeshift earthen ramp covering a portion of track. For transport, crewmen have removed the protruding machine guns, partially collapsed the conn, stowed a ready-to-use camouflage net on the upper rear and inserted a protective barrel tompion. Note the Roman numeral III between the side iron crosses. (NARA)

12

An immobilized Mark IV (male) serving as a dug-out's cover. Note the track 'spuds' and the penetration's irregular shape indicating the armour's hardness, but limited flexibility. (*Illustrated War News*)

Pozières Tank Memorial, marking where tanks first set off for combat on 15 September 1916. The surrounding barrier is made from early tank driving chains, and is supported by 6-pounder gun barrels. Displayed models are the Mark IV, Mark V, Mark I Gun-Carrier and Mark A Whippet. (Author)

## 1917

| | |
|---|---|
| **7 June** | Mark IVs are first used in combat at Messines Ridge. |
| **27 July** | Heavy Branch, British Machine Gun Corps, renamed the Tank Corps. |
| **29 September** | The Prussian War Ministry organizes the first A7V units. |
| **October (late)** | First A7V, 'Gretchen' (501), is completed. |
| **20 November** | 378 Mark IVs attack en masse in the Cambrai sector. |

## 1918

| | |
|---|---|
| **21 March** | A7Vs first used in combat near Saint-Quentin, as part of Operation *Michael*. |
| **24 April** | A7Vs and Mark IVs fight history's first tank-on-tank action at Villers-Bretonneux. |
| **22/23 June** | The Tank Corps conducts the first night action with armour at Bucquoy. |
| **4 July** | 60 British Whippets and new Mark Vs help take Hamel, alongside US forces, in the vehicles' combat debut. |
| **8 August** | 414 British and French tanks participate in the battle of Amiens, which precipitates a general German withdrawal in the West. |
| **8 October** | British Mark IVs fight captured German (*Beute*) Mark IVs in the Séranvillers–Niergnies–Awoingt area, south-east of Cambrai. |
| **11 October** | Final German use of A7Vs during World War I, at Iwuy, northeast of Cambrai. |
| **1 November** | Final *Beute* action at Sebourg. |

# DESIGN AND DEVELOPMENT

## MARK IV

In an effort to find a solution for how best to break the Western Front deadlock and reintroduce battlefield mobility, British designers, engineers and entrepreneurs concocted a variety of technological remedies that were frequently of little or no practical value. Tracked vehicles, however, showed promise in addressing the unique demands of contemporary front-line combat, and much of the developmental focus responded accordingly. Having struggled to sell their patented 'caterpillar' track (aka 'creeping grip') tractors domestically, Richard Hornsby & Sons of Lincolnshire sold the rights to the American Holt Manufacturing Company in 1911. The company, ironically, was later purchased by Britain to produce heavy artillery transports. While observing these prime movers in action on 19 October 1914, the British war correspondent Major Ernest Swinton considered the possibility of adapting them to more aggressive uses, of the sort that had been portrayed in H.G. Wells's 1903 science fiction short story, 'The Land Ironclads'.

Although he promoted the idea of a bulletproof tracked vehicle to Colonel Maurice Hankey (the Secretary of the Committee of Imperial Defence), Field Marshal John French and other senior British Army staff officers, the unconventional concept garnered little support. This was officially attributed to limited industrial capacity,

British ROD803 Rolls-Royce Armoured Car (1914 Pattern). The Royal Naval Air Service (RNAS) Armoured Car Division applied 6mm armour plating to a Rolls-Royce Silver Ghost passenger car chassis, which possessed excellent durability and cross-country capabilities. Armed with a turreted Maxim machine gun, it was used primarily for patrol duties. (Captain S. Walter)

and high estimated research and production costs, but also owed something to the fact that many of Swinton's contemporaries shared the assessment of the British Expeditionary Force's (BEF) Commander-in-Chief General Sir Douglas Haig: that machine guns were a 'much overrated weapon'. Tasked with creating 'special devices for the Western Front', Colonel Hankey and the First Lord of the Admiralty, Winston Churchill, showed more foresight. Motivated to find a 'mechanical remedy' to the 'mechanical danger' posed by machine guns and artillery, Churchill had toyed with several ideas to get forces across no-man's-land in relative safety. The employment of numerous smoke generators, various personal and vehicle-mounted shields, and even massive machine-gun-armed infantry combat tractors with articulated armoured segments, however, never seemed to offer a viable solution.

To examine the matter better, on 20 February 1915 Churchill quietly created a Landships Committee at the Admiralty. The project included select naval personnel, engineers and politicians, and was kept secret from the War Office, the Board of the Admiralty and the Treasury, as Churchill rightly felt their very conventional culture would stifle development of the unproven tank concept. After a month of debate members gravitated towards two designs, one with wheels and the other with tracks, and on 26 March Churchill personally provided £70,000 toward the development of six prototypes of the former, and 12 of the latter. As the tracked option proved superior for its intended use, William Foster & Co. Ltd's 105hp tractor was chosen as a power source. With development in secret soon undertaken, the largely female factory workforce was told they were creating 'water carriers destined for Mesopotamia', or more simply, 'tanks'.

In the expert hands of three men – William Tritton, his chief draughtsman/engineer William Rigby, and Royal Naval Air Service (RNAS) Lieutenant Walter Wilson – the British tank programme got under way at the company's Wellington Foundry just west of Lincoln. Some 37 days later, the team unveiled a 15-tonne tracked, boiler-plate-armoured box, which was then tested on unused factory property on 19 September 1915. Although the Director of Naval Construction approved this 'Number 1 Lincoln Machine' as having promise, its American chain-based tracks (made for the Bullock Tractor Company) were prone to dislodging, and were unsuited for mass production. Like most things related to this embryonic technology, there was no suitable replacement track on the market, and Tritton and Wilson feverishly worked on a solution at the Yarborough Suite (aka the 'Tank Room') of the nearby White Hart Hotel. After numerous flawed ideas, including the use of non-elastic balatá (natural latex) belts and flat wire ropes, the pair settled on unsprung chain links, with durable pressed steel plates that were riveted and hinged by pins. On completion of the prototype three days later, Tritton, representing the factory's other 'proud parents', informed the Admiralty of the arrival of 'Little Willie'.

In an effort to correct deficiencies in the initial design, an improved 28-tonne version was completed in an equally remarkable 141 days. Designed to have a low centre of gravity, sponsons were mounted to the sides, and tracks were wrapped round the vehicle in a rhomboid shape to provide maximum ground contact, with an angled front for negotiating obstacles. Known as 'Centipede', and 'Big Willie', after its combat debut the nickname 'Mother' stuck. Barring a 6-pounder cannon test misfire that nearly sent

# MARK IV SPECIFICATIONS

**General**

Production run (14 months from March 1917–May 1918): 1,220 (420 males, 595 females and 205 supply)

Combat weight: male: 28.4 tonnes, female: 27.4 tonnes

Crew: 8 (1 commanding officer, 7 enlisted (driver, 2 gunners and loader/machine-gunners, and 2 brakemen)

**Dimensions**

Length: 8m

Width: male: 4.11m, female 3.2m

Height: 2.43m

**Armour**

Conn front: 12mm @ 90 degrees

Conn sides: 8mm @ 90 degrees

Glacis: (upper) 12mm @ 45 degrees; (lower) 12mm @ 27 degrees; 12mm @ 24 degrees

Hull side: 8mm @ 90 degrees

Hull rear: 6mm @ 90 degrees

Hull deck: 6mm @ 0 degrees

Hull roof: 6mm @ 0 degrees

**Armament (male)**

Main guns: 2× Ordnance QF 6-pounder 305kg Hotchkiss Mk I or II (L/23) on mounting casemate special Mk 1

Main gun sight: 4× No. 4 Mk III sighting scope

Main gun ammunition: 332 (commonly 55 per cent high explosive; 40 per cent solid shot; 5 per cent canister)*

Main gun rate of fire: 20rd/min

Secondary armament: 3× air-cooled Lewis .303 machine guns (bow; one per sponson) plus one spare

Secondary ammunition: 5,640 rounds (40× 47-round drums per station)

**Armament (female)**

Main armament: 5× air-cooled Lewis guns (bow; two per sponson) plus one spare

**Motive power**

Engine: Daimler/Knight 105hp (78.3kW) @ 1,000rpm sleeve valve, straight-six cylinder, water cooled

Power/weight: 3.7hp/tonne

Transmission: two-speed primary box; one reverse; secondary two-speed selectors on the output shafts

Clutch: cone

Suspension: none (track rollers attached directly to frame)

Ignition: high-voltage magneto

Fuel capacity: 318l (petrol/gasoline)

Track width: 520mm

**Performance**

Ground pressure: 0.89kg/cm²

Maximum speed: 5.9km/h

Operational range: 56km

Fuel consumption: 5.9l/km

Fording: 1.8m

Step climbing: 1.4m

Climbing: 22 degrees

Trench crossing: 3.5m

Ground clearance: 0.5m

* Tank round ratios were not fixed, with combat circumstances generally dictating the mix.

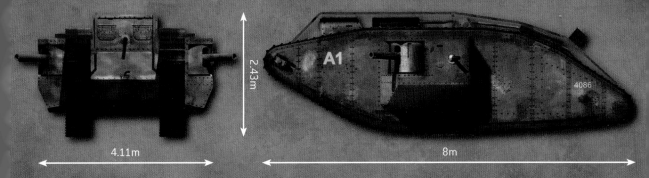

2.43m

4.11m

A1

4086

8m

## MARK IV (MALE) A1 (4086), 1ST BATTALION, 3RD TANK BRIGADE

Often mistakenly listed as '4066', a Mark IV that had been burned out on 22 March 1918, this is 2nd Lieutenant Frank Mitchell's tank in the colour scheme and markings likely to have been worn during the action at Villers-Bretonneux. Having abandoned the early disruptive 'Solomon' pattern of blotchy yellows, greys and browns as being too visible, British tankers' vehicles were soon painted in a uniform, dark-brown khaki that could be supplemented with

camouflage nets. On 16 April 1918 British tank crews were ordered to apply distinctive white–red–white national identification stripes to the side/front of their vehicles to differentiate them from increasing numbers of German *Beute* (Booty) Mark IVs. Along with adding white–red–white aircraft recognition marks on top of the cabs, however, such modifications had not been implemented on British armour fighting at Villers-Bretonneux.

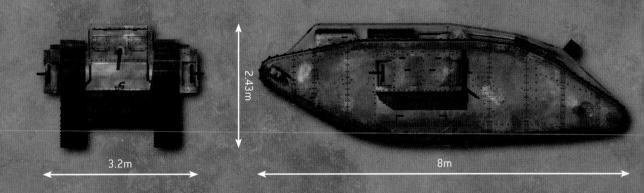

2.43m

3.2m

8m

## MARK IV (FEMALE), 1ST BATTALION, 3RD TANK BRIGADE

This unmarked Mark IV (female) represents a typical paint scheme for British service at the time of the German spring offensives in 1918. Like their male counterparts, females often displayed vehicle call-signs, serial numbers and four-digit identification numbers. Considering the potential for soft ground at the end of April, the unditching beam could prove beneficial.

One of the first tanks in combat, the Mark I (male) D20 'Daphne' (744) is pictured just after the Flers-Courcelette battle on 15 September 1916. The vehicle's camouflage scheme, designed by British artist Solomon Solomon, consisted of a medium-grey base overpainted with sand and brown blotches, and black outlines. (Geoffrey Malins)

a round into Lincoln Cathedral nearby, the platform was deemed acceptable and incorporated. With the British tank programme up and running, the members entrusted further efforts to a small executive supply committee, cover-named the Tank Supply Committee, whose recommendations were submitted directly to the Admiralty, the endeavour's champion. With the RNAS Armoured Car Division deactivated as the War Office assumed control of all land operations, Churchill retained control of its No. 20 Squadron for use in tank training, testing and evaluation. 'Mother' soon entered production as the Mark I. Although struggling through its combat debut, Haig remained very optimistic, and ordered a thousand vehicles to guarantee enough would be available for his next offensive. As the tank concept appeared to pay dividends, in spite of its mechanical and operational shortcomings, the Russian, French and Belgian governments clamoured for Britain to build tanks for them as well.

## PRODUCTION

As 150 Mark Is had proved that the design warranted continuation, the 100 vehicles still in the production queue were given minor improvements (including having their awkward steering tail wheels removed), and were used for training. Of these, two groups of 25 'males' (each armed with two cannon plus machine guns) and 25 'females' (machine guns only) were respectively designated Mark IIs (featuring wider track shoes and an increase in the thickness of the front and side plates to 10mm) and Mark IIIs (additional armour). In November 1916, the War Office ordered that an upgraded Mark IV combat model should enter production in March 1917, but after weeks of delays, it was decided several companies would participate. Standardization was understandably paramount as each firm constructed sub-assemblies before sending them to an erecting shop for final attachment.

The Metropolitan Carriage, Wagon & Finance Co. Ltd of Birmingham produced 640 Mark IV males and females as well as 180 converted supply tanks, while William Foster & Co. of Lincoln created 100 Mark IVs, as well as all Mark A Whippets. Supplemental work was undertaken by: Sir W.G. Armstrong, Whitworth & Co. Ltd (Newcastle-upon-Tyne) and Coventry Ordnance Works Ltd (100 males/ females each); William Beardmore & Co. Ltd of Glasgow (25 males and females plus 25 supply tanks); and Mirrlees, Bickerton & Day Ltd of Hazel Grove, near Manchester (50 females); meanwhile Ruston, Proctor & Co. (Lincoln) focused on producing male sponsons. By the war's end, some 1,220 Mark IVs had been produced (420 males, 595 females and 205 supply tanks). Each factory had its own testing grounds, as well as access to railway sidings and a marshalling yard.

Besides technical, design and doctrinal problems associated with producing and fielding tanks in sufficient numbers, and a frequently indifferent Army and related governmental departments, the British tank programme competed for raw materials and manufacturing resources with rail, aircraft, naval and munitions interests. Although by 1917 the vehicles were increasingly seen as a battlefield asset, civilian contractors were often more inclined to work on better-paid and less experimental contracts. Taken as a whole, such factors conspired to delay armoured vehicle production, and negate the incorporation of fundamental mechanical improvements, such as new engines and transmissions.

Owing to its box-like structure, the Mark IV was composed of inner and outer suspension frames that were riveted to their connecting panels, and manually installed at an erecting shop. After slotting the cast-iron track rollers to their respective fixed axles, the chassis was lowered onto the tracks, after which the gear wheels and drive sprockets were installed between the frames. The Daimler engine (the Daimler Motor Company Ltd had earlier been established in Britain, where it acquired the use of the German Daimler Motor Company's name and patents), gearbox, differential and control levers were then lined up on a sub-frame and installed, along with the radiator and fan assembly. Rear and roof plates were applied, followed by final fittings. A small escape hatch was provided in the roof, and the cab was narrowed to accommodate wider tracks (not available until 1918), while hinged, slitted visors were provided for the commander and brakeman, and top-mounted brackets for anchoring camouflage nets. In addition to remounting the exposed forward petrol tank to the rear, the Mark IV had thicker armour, and sponsons that could now be swung inside during rail transport, instead of having to be carried separately on trucks.

## LAYOUT

Like those of its predecessors, the Mark IV's forward compartment comprised a narrow shelf with padded seats for the commanding junior officer (port) and brakemen (starboard), while in between a round plugged ball mount was fitted for a forward-firing air-cooled Lewis gun. The commander was responsible for determining the route, watching for targets, and operating a clutch and brake in conjunction with the driver. Should rough terrain or route negotiation become a problem, the commander often left the tank to lead it on foot, usually with a makeshift staff to test the path's suitability. At night it was not uncommon for the commander to hold a lighted cigarette behind him so the brakeman could maintain visual contact. When not needed for steering, the commander could also stand on the gearbox cover behind the engine to observe the tank's external surroundings in relative safety. Regarded as the vehicle's most skilled – and valuable – crewmember, the brakeman was responsible for navigation, as well as operating and maintaining the second change speed brake for each track. Amidships, each sponson had a main gunner, and a loader/machine-gun operator (two machine guns for female sponsons), but unlike previous models, the Mark IV (male) had no ammunition stowage beneath the gun. Two brakemen were stationed on each side of the tank, to operate the tracks' secondary gearboxes, as well as distribute ammunition, grease and oil machinery, and operate machine guns if needed.

One of the six Mark IV (male) tanks, 'Nelson' (130), used as 'Tank Banks' to promote government War Bonds and War Savings Certificate sales by touring England, Wales and Scotland in 1918. (H.D. Girdwood)

## VARIANTS

Older Mark I–IVs were commonly transformed into supply tanks, which provided 'fills' for up to five tanks – 91l of water, 273l of petrol, 45l of oil, 4.5kg of grease, 10,000 rounds of small-arms ammunition for a female, and 200 6-pounder and 6,000 small-arms rounds for a male. Occasionally, Mark IV supply tanks were converted back into fighting varieties, and from September 1917 many were provided with rudimentary wireless sets. Other versions experimented with using mortars placed between the rear horns, or recovery gear or grapnels to clear paths through wire; an important asset considering it commonly took twenty times the artillery man-hours to reduce a section of trenches and wire entanglements as it did to prepare them. To improve trench-crossing capabilities, an extended chassis and rear track horns that resembled a tadpole tail were tried, but were found too awkward for combat use.

In addition to tank conversions, Central Workshops produced several field modifications, including sledges for carrying armour-related supplies, and towing gear.

While covering retreating British infantry on 23 March 1918, 5th Battalion's Mark IV males (4056) and (8043) were deemed too wide to cross the Brie Bridge over the river Somme. Although Royal Engineers allowed the female (2741) passage before the structure was demolished, the pair, and the remaining vehicles (2811 at right, 4659, 2331, and 2781) were subsequently burned and abandoned. (NARA)

A top-mounted brushwood fascine, 1.4m in diameter by 3m long, could be attached, to assist in crossing wider trenches, such as the 4–5m versions encountered on the Hindenburg Line. Comprised of 100–150 normal fascines, tightly bound by two tanks pulling chains in opposite directions, the result could be dropped via a release gear into a trench or water obstruction, thus allowing the vehicle to cross. Hexagonal timber frameworks reinforced with 610kg steel were produced for similar uses. For moving through exceptionally soft terrain, a 4m-long,

457kg, iron-tipped oak unditching beam could be employed. First used with Mark IVs, it was chain-anchored to rails along the tank's upper structure, and when needed two crewmen climbed onto the vehicle and attached it to the tracks using spanners, where it acted as a large, traction-assisting grouser. Once freed from such terrain, the beam would be returned to its original position.

# A7V

Although the British combat debut of tanks near Bois d'Elville (Delville Wood) – part of the Flers-Courcelette (Somme) fight on 15 September 1916 – produced mixed physical results due to breakdowns, inexperienced crews, rough terrain and limited numbers of machines, the detrimental psychological effects on their enemy were considerable. German intelligence had gleaned fragmentary evidence that their adversary was developing such a weapon system, but having been subjected to its reality the previously unconcerned OHL (Oberste Heeresleitung, or Supreme Army Command) lobbied the War Ministry to develop an equivalent. Like many of their British, French, Austro-Hungarian and Russian counterparts, German senior commanders generally remained sceptical of the fledgling tank concept. Having developed elastic, defence-in-depth techniques to erode Allied strength along the operationally deadlocked Western Front, most put stock in adaptive counters such as forward-positioned artillery and mortars in direct-fire roles, and armour-piercing bullets, such as those used against enemy sniper loopholes. German industry had recently initiated a major streamlining of armaments production, as part of the Hindenburg Programme, so relevant firms were often reluctant to divert increasingly limited resources to developing new, unproven technologies such as tracked/armoured combat vehicles.

Originally produced as a 'female', A7V 'Mephisto' (506) has the open sight cut-out above the breech hole for the ad hoc incorporation of one of the four *Bocklafette* 57mm cannon. Note the devil carrying away a British tank. (Shane Black, courtesy of Queensland Museum)

The German authorities had toyed with creating domestic armour for several years, but beyond the promise shown early in the war by armoured cars and tracked artillery prime movers, many maintained an anachronistic belief that wheels and horses were respectively best suited for road and cross-country duties. As the war progressed, however, the need for an off-road combat and supply/personnel transport increased. The War Ministry responded by promoting the development of a solution. Although the Ministry oversaw all armament production, power was shared among the administrations of 21 Prussian and three Bavarian army corps, plus a Guard corps, each responsible for maintaining a front-line corps in addition to equivalent reserve and Landwehr (territorial reserve) corps. To minimize friction between the military administration and command camps, a field motor transport service chief was created, but problems persisted. The War Ministry's *Kriegsrohstoff-Abteilung* (War Raw Materials Section), which tried to control and coordinate numerous private industries contributing to the war effort, was frequently at odds with the latter's capitalist and/or autonomous motivations. Regarding the development of German armour, this was illustrated by the lack of enthusiasm the VPK (*Verkehrstechnischen Prüfungskommission* – Traffic Technical Examination Commission) received when attempting to garner support from various automotive, engineering and manufacturing firms. Combined with the fact that what limited quantities of fuel were available were being priority-allocated to the *Luftstreitkräfte* (Air Force), U-boat forces and essential motorized transport, the German tank programme appeared stillborn.

Undeterred, on 13 November 1916, the War Ministry contracted the VPK to develop a 30-tonne *Panzerkampfwagen* (armoured fighting vehicle), which in turn allocated *Allgemeines Kriegsdepartement, 7.Abteilung, Verkehrswesen* (General War Department, 7th Section, Transport) to bring the idea to fruition. Hauptmann (Reserve) Joseph Vollmer (the founder of the German Automobile Construction Company) was chosen as the new department head because of his considerable experience in automotive design and engineering. Adhering to the War Ministry, A2 (Infantry Department) requirements that the new vehicle (cover-named A7V after its development section) should possess a front- and a rear-mounted quick-firing cannon, six machine guns and an ability to carry a small assault infantry contingent, Vollmer presented initial designs to the Army on 22 December 1916. The stipulation that it also have artillery-resistant 30mm armour all round was not worth the commensurate weight increase, and ultimately this thickness was only applied to the vehicle's front, while other areas were protected by 20mm or less. To make the most of limited resources, the A7V's chassis was to be designed to accommodate a prime mover/transport, or *Überlandwagen* (cross-country wagon). As the British rhomboid shape and side-mounted sponsons were unsuited for such a dual-purpose framework, the latter's superstructure would resemble a simple flat-car with a central driver's position, while the combat version resembled an armoured blockhouse. Holt caterpillar tracks were incorporated via a licence with the company's Austro-Hungarian subsidiary in Budapest. Vollmer promised a functioning prototype within five months, so an optimistic VPK ordered a run of 100 vehicles that later included ten armoured A7Vs.

On 12 April 1917 the Germans captured a Mark II just west of Cambrai, the first of many British tanks to be taken, and although it helped focus interest on the development of a domestic equivalent, attention to the A7V programme was frequently affected by teething troubles. Just four days later the disastrous introduction of French tanks near Berry-au-Bac, and their subsequent nicknaming as 'rolling crematoria', did little to alleviate OHL's or Chief General Quartermaster Erich Ludendorff's scepticism about the concept. Although development of the A7V would continue, questions arose as to whether resources were being best allocated. Its own Operations Section II head, Oberstleutnant Max Bauer, pushed for more easily produced light tanks, while others stressed scrapping the A7V, and simply relying on reused *Beute* (booty) tanks or direct copies.

Having constructed a wooden-armoured A7V mock-up (No. 500) in mid-January, on 30 April, Daimler Motors Company unveiled a functional A7V prototype at its test track in the Berlin suburb of Marienfelde. The vehicle's tendency to throw tracks, and a poor demonstration over obstacles that simulated a battlefield in front of a high-ranking audience, however, prompted Ludendorff's lackey, the Minister of War, Hermann von Stein, to call for its use only in a defensive capacity. On 14 May 1917, a second demonstration at Mainz, with no main gun and 10 tonnes of ballast that simulated the proposed armour's weight, made a better showing. An unarmoured production A7V was completed four months later, and it was subsequently sent to the Geländefahrschule (cross-country driving school) at Zossen (Berlin) for trials.

A7V 'Mephisto' (506)'s starboard access door illustrates the different paint variations the vehicle has received since arriving in Australia in 1919. The components above and below the handle are part of the interior handle locks, while the disc covers a viewing hole. (Shane Weier, courtesy of Queensland Museum)

## PRODUCTION

In December 1917 it was decided that several companies would create component parts for the A7V, including Daimler (Marienfelde), producing engines; Adler Works (Frankfurt am Main), for gears; Brass & Herstett (Marienfelde), for chassis; Caterpillar-Holt (Budapest), for tracks; Oberursel Motor Factory (Oberursel), for radiators; Berlin-Anhalt Works (Berlin), for machinery equipment; and Friedrich Krupp Corporation (Essen) and Röchling Iron and Steelworks, LLC (Dillinger Hütte), for armour plating. Although Vollmer had secured three firms to provide final assembly, Büssing Corporation (Braunschweig), and Loeb Works Corporation (Berlin-Charlottenburg) eventually withdrew, citing production constraints, which left Daimler to the task. Heinrich Lanz Corporation (Mannheim) was to develop the A7V's tracked tractor, with armour plates assembled by Steffens and Nölle Corporation (Berlin-Tempelhof), a firm that constructed girders and bridges.

In addition to general lack of enthusiasm in establishing a German tank programme, raw-material shortages, transport delays and workforce disruptions caused by wartime personnel needs and growing labour unrest hampered rapid A7V production. The considerable amount of hand crafting and fitting that was necessary produced construction inaccuracies and variations in components, including exhaust pipes, flaps, mudguards, hinges, tow hooks, door seats and machine-gun apertures and mounts. The A7V's under-strength chassis often needed to be reinforced post-production, just to get the ungainly design to operate over terrain that was relatively flat, open and firm. Its gears were hard to shift, engines often overheated on starting, and the clutches risked burning out from stresses encountered by the tracks when they became entangled in obstacles such as barbed wire. The front-mounted cannon's limited 90-degree coverage created a visibility gap with the forward machine guns, which meant that the driver had to compensate by moving in a zigzag motion to prevent exploitation of the weakness.

The A7V's front and rear hinged tow hooks were armour-protected to resist damage and snagging, while a low-mounted horizontal plate helped compensate for the unarmoured underbody. Access doors were provided at the port front and starboard rear, and a round escape hatch was added below the stern plate. An armoured panel

# A7V SPECIFICATIONS

## General
Production run (6 months, October 1917–April 1918 ): 20
Combat weight: 29.9 tonnes (armour 8.5 tonnes; weapons/
   ammunition 3.5 tonnes; crew/equipment 2 tonnes)
Crew: 18 (two officers: commander, driver, 16 enlisted:
   mechanic, mechanic/signaller, 12 infantrymen
   (6 machine-gunners, 6 loaders), 2 artillerymen:
   main gunner, loader, plus up to 8 assault infantry

## Dimensions*
Length: 7.35m
Width: 3.06m
Height: 3.35m

## Armour
Conn: (front/rear) 15mm @ 75 degrees; (sides) 15mm
   @ 80 degrees
Glacis: (upper) 30mm @ 85 degrees; (lower) 30mm
   @ 47 degrees
Hull side: 20mm @ 80 degrees
Hull rear: (upper) 20mm @ 85 degrees; (lower) 20mm
   @ 47 degrees
Hull bottom: 10mm @ 0 degrees
Hull roof: 6mm @ 10 degrees

## Armament
Main gun (first type): QF 57mm Cockerill-Nordenfelt
   casemate (L/26.3) horizontal (90 degrees); vertical
   (± 20 degrees)
Main gun sight (first type): 4× CP Goerz Rundblick-Fernrohr
   (RblF) 16 (panoramic telescope)
Main gun (second type): QF 57mm Maxim-Nordenfelt
   casemate (L/26.3) horizontal (90 degrees); vertical
   (± 20 degrees)
Main gun sight (second type): Open sights (notch
   and bead)

Main gun ammunition: 180 (official)–300 rounds
   (commonly 50 per cent canister; 30 per cent armour
   piercing; 20 per cent high explosive)**
Main gun rate of fire: 20rd/min
Secondary armament: 6× water-cooled 7.92mm MG 08,
   plus one spare MG 08/15
Secondary ammunition: 15,000 rounds (10× 250-round
   boxes per station)

## Motive power
Engine: 2× Daimler 165-204 100hp (200hp total) (74.6kW
   each) @ 800rpm 4-cylinder, water-cooled engines, with
   a Pallas carburettor rpm limiter
Power/weight: 6.7hp/tonne
Transmission: mechanical three-speed, maximum 3km/h,
   6km/h and 10km/h (same for reverse)
Clutch: cone
Suspension: helical spring
Ignition: high-voltage magneto
Fuel capacity: 2×250l (petrol/benzene mix)
Track width: 500mm

## Performance
Ground pressure: 0.69kg/cm²
Maximum speed: 16km/h road; 8km/h cross-country
Operational range: 60–70km road; 30–35km cross-country
Fuel consumption: 7.5l/km road; 16l/km cross-country
Fording: 0.8m
Step climbing: 0.4m
Climbing: 25 degrees
Trench crossing: 2m
Ground clearance: 0.4m
* There were minor variations among individual vehicles.
** Tank round ratios were not fixed, with combat
circumstances generally dictating the mix.

## A7V 'BADEN I' (505), ATD 3/GROUP II

'Baden I' (505) was part of Röchling's initial batch of five A7Vs, and originally had a *Bocklafette* (trestle gun carriage) mount, before being fitted with the less ad hoc *Sockellafette* (pedestal gun carriage). It lacked the conn appliqué armour that was added to ATD 2 vehicles, as well as door seats. The A7V participated in the actions at Saint-Quentin (March 1918), Villers-Bretonneux (April), the Matz River (June) and Saint-Etienne (October), and was only taken after the war at Ebenheim, Germany.

Starting in 1917 the German Army tested various vehicle camouflage schemes beyond the standard white and bright yellows and blues, earth tones, and the ambiguously defined *Feldgrau*. The first ten A7V tanks were painted a green-grey colour that apparently resembled cut grass. In preparation for Ludendorff's planned Peace Offensive, some tank commanders had additional camouflage applied to their vehicles as they passed through Charleroi for maintenance. These generally followed an unofficial pattern of clay-yellow, red-brown and pale-green splotches. Individual commanders also named their vehicles, while those from ATD 1 had distinguishing white skulls framed by black backgrounds. *Beute* Mark IVs that had passed through Charleroi received a greenish base coat, over which similar paint schemes were applied. Both types had iron crosses applied to their sides, fronts, rear, and – for aerial identification – to the roof.

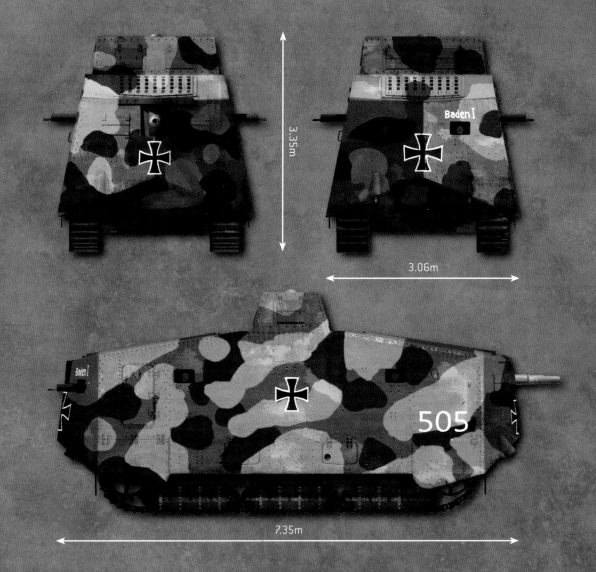

3.35m

3.06m

7.35m

could be removed to give access to the low-mounted front idler wheel and the rear drive sprocket, and ten armour-shuttered visors (two front, two rear and one per side for the cupola, plus two front and one per side for the hull) enabled the crew, or accompanying assault infantry, to use small arms or grenades. Heat- and fume-dissipating roof ventilation louvres were positioned fore and aft, with a generator producing electricity for internal and external lights.

## LAYOUT

The A7V's size and mechanical complexity required a crew of 16 men and two officers to operate at full effectiveness. The vehicle's forward fighting compartment comprised the 26.3-calibre Quick Firing (QF) 57mm Cockerill-Nordenfelt casemate cannon manned by a gunner, with a loader to his right. One 60-round ammunition container was positioned on the floor just ahead of the forward radiator, and one each near the port and starboard two-person machine-gun positions. Although officially carrying 180 rounds, crews often carried up to double that amount, depending on the situation. Machine-gun ammunition was stored in low-backed, three-tiered padded seats that held up to ten Type 15 wooden cases, each containing a 250-round woven cotton belt with brass spacers. Front and rear mechanics occupied oval-backed seats in front of each radiator, to perform regular engine maintenance and monitoring.

The central section contained the tank's engine, with a narrow walkway along either side to facilitate movement throughout the vehicle. Some 1.6m above the deck, the commander sat to the driver's front right, within an armoured conn. To turn, the driver could alter the speed of one engine in relation to the other using a large horizontal hand-wheel, while a pair of foot clutches were provided at the floorboard, which had a diamond pattern for grip. A left-hand lever controlled the brake/supplementary steering, while on his right was a double-lever quadrant. The outer levers operated that

A7V 'Mephisto' (506)'s rear machine-gun mounts, tow hook cover and round escape hatch, photographed in 1989 at the Queensland Museum, Brisbane, Australia. The vehicle was subsequently moved to a glass enclosure. (Shane Black, courtesy of Queensland Museum)

side's track, and the inner ones controlled the three gears, set for 3km/h, 6km/h and 12km/h, plus neutral. One reverse lever for each engine was also available. An additional hand-wheel started the engines. If one would not turn over, releasing the clutch on the operating engine could lurch the vehicle forward and force an ignition. Unlike those of the British Marks I–IV, the A7V's driver could perform all the physical work related to his duties. The cab possessed a pair of top-mounted hatches, and its armoured panels could be partially collapsed for rail transport. Although visibility from the conn was acceptable, the machine's extended front and rear blocked what the driver could see in these directions inside a 9m arc, so the mechanics frequently communicated corrections by observing their vehicle's movements via side hatches, or while sitting on the folding door plate. The A7V's rear compartment reflected the front, except for a pair of MG 08 machine guns in place of a main gun.

## VARIANTS

The *Überlandwagen* transport variety possessed a top speed of 13km/h and was operated by a driver and an assistant, located above the engine compartment. Sharing a common chassis with the A7V, it had poor cross-country performance that was further handicapped by lengthy cargo decks, and wooden dropsides. Loads often shifted during off-road driving, which risked damaging the radiators and tailboards, and its 10l/km fuel consumption was excessive, especially compared to something like an Albion A10 3-tonne lorry's expenditure of less than one-tenth the amount. A canopy was fitted over the driving position, which had swivelling seats, and duplicated rear controls for driving in either direction without having to turn the vehicle. Three Krupp-converted K-Flak guns were also tested in anti-aircraft roles on modified *Überlandwagen*; one with 2× German 77mm Sockelflak, and two with captured Russian Sockelflak 02s. As these vehicles were based on the tank's chassis, some were eventually converted to lightly armoured *Sturmpanzerwagen*, such as A7V 'Hedi', which was later used by government-backed Freikorps to quell the 1919 Communist-instigated Spartacist Uprising in Berlin.

*Überlandwagen* from Armee-Kraftwagen-Kolonne (Raupe) (Army Motor Vehicle Convoy (Tracked)) No. 1111 during testing near Wavrin, France, in March 1918. Note the swastika within a white octagon tactical symbol. (NARA)

# TECHNICAL
# SPECIFICATIONS

## MARK IV

### ARMOUR

Given that Britain possessed the world's largest navy in 1914, related armour and armament manufacturing capabilities were commensurate. Like their German adversaries, however, the British found that producing vehicle-sized equivalents necessitated retooling machinery, and developing expertise. The Mark I proved insufficiently protected against the new Mauser-fired 7.92mm K (*Kern*, or 'core') bullet, with its hardened alloy-steel centre that was surprisingly potent when loaded backward into the cartridge. The Parkhead works of William Beardmore & Co., Glasgow, therefore tested various explosives and ammunition against several qualities of steel before settling on nickel-steel plate, which had the necessary flexibility and toughness, as well as the light weight needed for easier construction. As 6mm and 8mm armour was resistant to weight-detonated explosives, normal bullets and Mills bombs respectively, the improved Mark IV was allocated armour of between 10mm and 12mm thickness. The latter was bullet-resistant up to a distance of 100m, as proved by the company, which tested their product with appropriate rifle fire before final approval.

# MARK IV (MALE) AMMUNITION

Through differential tempering, the 6-pounder cast solid-steel round (**1**) had a hardened tip to assist armour penetration, and a softer body that better maintained integrity during impact. It was 215mm long and weighed 2.72kg, had two copper driving bands, a slight swell at its ogival base to centre the loaded projectile, and a Class A copper alloy Hotchkiss Base Fuse Mk III, with a 115g fulminate bursting charge (FG Powder). All fuses were stamped with a number and mark, the makers' initials, date of manufacture, filling company's initials, date of filling and a lot number. The shell displayed a cartridge mark, type, charge, manufacturer and production date. Its cartridge case contained a 220g Cordite Mk I Size 5 charge. The round was painted black to indicate it was armour-piercing; practice rounds had a yellow band around the body.

The common shell (**2**), an Amatol explosive, with black letters on a green band listed the percentages of TNT and ammonium nitrate. It had a Mk III fuze (percussion), while its cartridge case had a 213g Cordite MD (Modified) Size 4.5 (a) charge. The shell was painted black, with a 12.7mm white and red 'explosive' band just below the tip, and its cartridge case's base was painted yellow with red stencilling. Practice rounds had a yellow band around the body.

The 6-pounder anti-personnel case (**3**), weighing 2.92kg, contained 80 sawdust-suspended, hardened lead balls. To increase the dispersion cone, the thin steel tube body incorporated six longitudinal grooves that promoted fracturing, and the upper end was crimped into a recess in the solid conical brass head. Both it, and the 57mm variety, had a range of some 300m.

The brass 57mm×306mmR bottlenecked cartridge shared by these three projectiles was used with the Mark I's longer 6-pounder (405kg) barrels, as well as those of the 305kg variety, but with a reduced propellant loading, shown by the latter having its lower half coloured with a bronzing liquid to differentiate it. Once struck with a firing pin its No. 2 Mk IV percussion primer detonated a Mk III Cordite MD charge, which had been wrapped in silk sewings to help stabilize the extruded cords of nitro-cellulose/nitro-glycerine smokeless propellant. Cartridge case bases were stamped with information including the gun type, lot number, manufacturer, whether loaded with a Cordite, CF/CR ('charge full' or 'charge reduced'), service ('L' for 'Land') and date of manufacture. Cases that had been fired, refurbished, annealed and reused received an additional 'F' or 'R' per iteration, while any original data was barred out and fresh data stamped.

1

2

3

British tank armour, like that of German manufacture, had its share of rejected plates, but the greater access to the necessary raw materials enjoyed by the British gave them the advantage of consistent production on a large scale. To avoid over-hardening the armour, Beardmore cast alternate layers of hard and soft steel, which was then rolled or forged. To strengthen the already cut plates, each underwent quench hardening, in which it was heated and immersed in oil, water or molten sodium cyanide. By not heating completely through the plate, it retained a face hardened front, and a strong back. As the Mark I's side sponsons were prone to catching on the ground, and needed to be removed for rail transport, those on the Mark IV were reduced, and bevelled at the bottom. This involved fully elevating the gun, so the barrel moved all the way back, unbolting the sponsons and swinging them inboard one end at a time, to be secured by a pin-and-clevis arrangement to the main engine bearers. The secondary gears, however, could only be operated if the sponson doors were lifted off their hinges and stowed separately. Because of the smaller space the Mark IV – unlike the Mark I – did not have ammunition racks under the sponson.

## ARMAMENT

Having the same naval lineage as the 57mm Nordenfelt QF cannon, the 6-pounder Hotchkiss version was incorporated into the initial Mark I tank design. Licence-built by the Elswick Ordnance Co. (an Armstrong-Whitworth subsidiary), its lengthy L/40 406kg single tube proved susceptible to damage by trees and the ground when operating over rough terrain. As a result, the Mark IV was allocated a lighter 305kg alternative, which was reinforced with a breech ring shrunk over its rear, and shortened by 112.7mm. On 19 January 1917, a built-up Mark II main gun, with a thicker, stiffer recoil-absorbing breech, was introduced, which used the same ammunition. Although this change marginally decreased range and initial muzzle velocity (411m/s), considering the close ranges at which tanks of this period operated, it was of minimal consequence.

The 6-pounder cannon was secured to a pedestal by a sliding crosshead that allowed pivoting on top of a trunnion. Elevation and traverse were controlled by hand, with recoil limited by hydraulic buffers. For targeting, gunners relied on No. 4 Mk III versions of sighting scopes, such as those made by Troughton & Simms Ltd (London); their 1916 model comprised a rotating eyepiece for focusing, and a fixed, 4× magnification. The commander coordinated vehicle activities using speaking tubes, which led to the brakeman and each sponson. A fire-control instrument operated by the commanding officer provided additional assistance by synchronizing his viewing direction with the respective gunner. In Quick Fire systems, the charge was contained in a metal cartridge case, which expanded on firing. Should a shell malfunction or not fire, it could be removed after a pause and ditched through the bottom of the sponson door.

Mark IV (male) 'Excellent' (2324), housed at the Tank Museum, Bovington, Dorset, showing its starboard ammunition ready racks, and sponson mantlet (right). The selector gear and hand pump (left and right), and second starboard change speed brake are seen with red handles around the commander's seat. The silver container just behind is one of two track oil tanks. (Stephen Pope, courtesy of the Tank Museum, Bovington)

The air-cooled Lewis gun provided a lightweight (13kg) weapon that was suited for the tank's cramped interior as it required minimal mounting, but it also suffered from overheating and fouling after prolonged use. Although it was housed in a rather large solid-steel ball/sight aperture within a phosphor bronze mounting, when the gun was removed the ball could be rotated inwards to eliminate a hull opening. When the Lewis gun was in use, the weapon tended to blow heated by-products like cordite fumes back at the user, because the tank's cooling fan drew air in from outside. Its encompassing aluminium radiator allowed the barrel to give off considerable heat as expelled gases produced a draught that sucked in cool air from the rear toward the muzzle. A shell deflector, with a catcher bag, could be added to contain the hot, spent cartridges that emerged from its corrugated 47-round circular steel magazine.

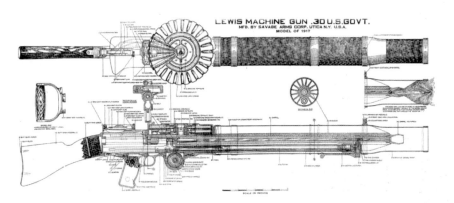

LEWIS MACHINE GUN .30 U.S.GOVT.
MFD. BY SAVAGE ARMS CORP. UTICA N.Y. U.S.A.
MODEL OF 1917

A German 225kg steam drop-hammer being used at an Army maintenance facility for lighter repairs, such as straightening axles. (NARA)

## MOBILITY

Like its predecessor, the Mark IV possessed a dated 105hp Daimler six-cylinder engine, although a limited number were mated to the more reliable and powerful 125hp upgrades, with aluminium pistons, twin carburettors, and faster rpm. Ignition was provided by a high-voltage alternating-current magneto electric generator. The rear-positioned drive passed from the engine though a cone clutch, incorporated within the flywheel, into a gearbox with two speeds and reverse, and gear-change handles. This configuration allowed the brakeman to shift without assistance, and should the carburettor malfunction, hand-feeding petrol directly into the engine using a rubber tube was an option, albeit a dangerous one. Power was then directed into a large worm differential casing, from which the drive passed, via a chain, to the rear-mounted driving sprocket.

Turning necessitated signalling to the gearsman in the rear to put the secondary gear on one side in neutral – an operation requiring synchronized timing and experience. The brakeman's foot pedal operated a band on the tail-shaft from the gearbox, which carried a worm that drove the crown wheel of a large reduction gear. This also served as a differential, enabling the track-driving wheels to rotate at different speeds when steering the tank on its track brakes. Once the differential locked, the gear became solid, removing the risk of one of the tracks slipping in poor terrain, thus risking falling sideways into a trench. Iron 'spuds' were also used to improve traction.

The Mark IV was relatively easy to maintain, and as it used the pre-war Foster-Daimler tractor, it offered a known mechanical arrangement. Wilson pushed for an engine improvement, but the head of the Mechanical Warfare Department, Major Albert Stern, was against the idea, and it was not until March 1917 that the decision was reversed following trials at Oldbury – too late for inclusion on the Mark IV. British tank engines ran at a relatively constant speed, governed mechanically at around 1,200rpm. Developing filters proved difficult, as the tracks threw up dust and mud that inevitably got inside. Travelling over angles placed considerable demands on the fuel and oil system, which had to ensure an adequate supply to the engine at all times to avoid parts seizing up or shutting down. To counter this problem, an electric Autovac vacuum pump fed fuel to the engine regardless of the vehicle's orientation. As its noisy operation could be heard as far as 500m away, artillery and low-flying aircraft were often used to mask the sounds.

Though German and French tanks had sprung suspensions that enabled greater speed, British models did not. This hampered their ability to negotiate challenging terrain, although it proved something of an asset in that it meant that during operation a tank could keep pace over suitable ground with accompanying infantry. After mid-1918, once more open battlefield environments were encountered, the Mark IV proved unsuited to missions involving rapid penetration and exploitation.

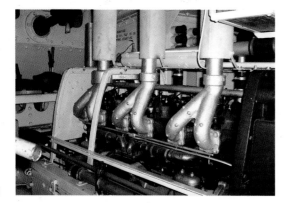

Daimler engine from 'Excellent', with its three vertical exhaust manifolds. (Stephen Pope, courtesy of the Tank Museum, Bovington)

# MARK IV SPONSON INTERIOR

1.  Upper recoil/recuperator cylinder
2.  Falling wedge breech block
3.  Breech shield
4.  Trigger/grip
5.  Lower recoil/recuperator
    cylinders
6.  Gun mount
7.  Mantlet
8.  Water container
9.  4× No. 4 Mk III sighting scope
10. Pistol ports
11. Machine gun mount
12. Access door
13. Manoeuvring rod
14. Loading/extracting handle
15. Vision port
16. Light

# A7V

## ARMOUR

In the half-century after the introduction of wrought-iron-protected wooden warships (ironclads) in the late 1850s, manufacturing techniques and naval armour quality improved, as carbon was introduced to produce steel of considerable strength. As increasing the amount of carbon beyond about 2 per cent hardened the metal to brittleness, making it unsuited for armour plate, other elements were incorporated, in varying amounts, to counter or enhance the metal depending on its intended use. These elements could include copper and chromium (for corrosion resistance); manganese (hardness); molybdenum and vanadium (strength and stability); and nickel (strength). Once war broke out in 1914, German firms with a history of arms production, such as Krupp Arms Works (Essen), and Röchling Iron and Steel Works (Saarland), were given the task of developing vehicle-mounted armour plate that was resistant to shrapnel, standard small arms and machine guns. Although capable of producing such plate, which was then face hardened – a process in which one side was treated with carbon-inducing charcoal or heated hydrocarbon gas – the A7V would not have the benefit of pressed armour that had been made externally hard, yet internally tough and resilient. The low priority of the German tank programme meant it had to settle for mild, nickel-deficient rolled or sheet iron boiler plate, which under 30mm thick, was subject to structural distortions, difficulty in machining, and had a propensity to crack, tear and/or split along the metal's fibres when hit by high-velocity projectiles. Continuing with Newton's third law of motion, projectile impacts commonly forced shale – metal flakes – and paint fragments to spray the vehicle's interior, causing casualties.

As it was optimal to add elements to steel plate in a controlled manner, simply melting, reheating and reforming deformed pieces was not an effective solution. Krupp's production of half of the initial ten A7V armour for chassis 508–512 (plus 513–515) reflected these problems. As an experimental AKK (Raupe) (Armee-Kraftwagen-Kolonne (Raupe), or Army Motor Vehicle Convoy (Tracked)) had been formed in September 1917, the eight frames were developed into *Überlandwagen* for the unit, while eight more (516–523) were assigned to AKK (Raupe) 1112. A7Vs 503, 504, 541, 542 and 543 had their defective Krupp plates cut and straightened prior to installation. The resulting nine sections – five side, two front and two rear – were then bolted into place, as contemporary welding practices were rudimentary, and unsuited to assembling tank armour. Röchling's armour, similarly deficient in strengthening elements, did not require post-production modification, and vehicles 501, 505, 506 and 507, plus 502 (hull)/540 (chassis), had single front/side/rear sections. The remaining ten A7V plates (525–529 and 560–564) were produced by both manufacturers.

## ARMAMENT

Although the first A7Vs appeared in October 1917, it took until spring 1918 to find a suitable main gun. Initially, German planners considered an eight-embrasure, interchangeable mounting design incorporating a pair of lightweight 20mm Becker TuF (*Tank und Flieger* – tank and air) automatic cannons, and 4–6 MG 08 machine guns

A detail of A7V (506) 'Mephisto's' three-bogie suspension, with each comprised of five wheels, three return rollers, and supported by springs (two front and rear, and four in the centre), which provided a degree of support over rough terrain. The side flaps allowed access to powertrain components. Note the simple exhaust hole (vehicles 501, 505, 506, 507, and 540), instead of a pipe. (Shane Weier, courtesy of Queensland Museum)

and/or flamethrowers, although the latter were abandoned as they sucked the air out of the tank, and could set fire to on-board oil and petrol containers. With the Becker's low muzzle velocity, and limited magazine capacity for its armour-piercing and incendiary rounds, it was also eliminated from contention. Krupp's limited-range, high-recoil M1896 77mm field cannon was also unsuited for cramped operation, and although the modernized M1916 had proven successful against tanks as part of *Nahkampf-Batterien* (close combat batteries), they were in very limited supply.

Having appropriated numerous Belgian-made 57mm *Caponnière* (casemate) cannon, of which some 150 were reused as truck-mounted anti-tank guns following Cambrai, the Germans opted to incorporate the Belgian weapon into the A7V. Originally intended in the late 19th century to counter torpedo boats that incorporated thicker armour and reinforced coal bunkers, these quick-firing, fixed ammunition systems were developed by ordnance industrialists such as Thorsten Nordenfelt and Benjamin B. Hotchkiss. The former, having sold his company to Hiram Maxim in 1888, soon breached his contract with the new Maxim-Nordenfelt Guns and Ammunition Company, evaded an agreement not to compete for 25 years, and established another arms-manufacturing company with headquarters in Paris; this new firm was fronted by Nordenfelt's relatives to retain the family name. In October 1890, Nordenfelt joined with the John Cockerill Company (Seraing, Belgium), which subsequently produced the 'new' 57mm QF 26.3-calibre design. The Belgian authorities purchased 185 examples to equip the renovated fortifications around Namur, Liege, Huy, Antwerp and elsewhere. In this capacity, they were to clear enemy infantry from forward defensive positions, which necessitated the predominant use of canister.

# A7V AMMUNITION

The 57mm *Kanonen-Granate 16 (1916) mit Panzerkopf* (shot) (**1**) provided the A7V with a dedicated 3.1kg anti tank projectile that combined a high-explosive shell with an armour-piercing head. As a wartime expedient, this was simply the KGr 15 (1915) high-explosive round, with a screwed-on, hardened steel ogive (head), and three copper driving bands to help position it within the cannon's rifled barrel. To assist in penetrating face-hardened enemy tank armour, the semi-armour-piercing projectile had an aluminium percussion fuse that was activated by the discharge shock, and triggered on impact via a *Granatfüllung 88* (picric acid) charge. This detonated a 0.12kg *Füllpulver 60/40* (filling powder) Amatol bursting charge made up of 60 per cent TNT (trinitrotoluene) and 40 per cent ammonium nitrate, which as an oxidising agent intensified an explosion, and lessened the need for limited quantities of TNT. As with other artillery rounds, paint was used to minimize rust and corrosion, and indicate its type. The all-black round had a brownish-red head, with roughly one-third possessing a smoke-generating charge of 90 per cent red phosphorus or arsenic and 10 per cent paraffin/kerosene to enhance impact visibility.

The 57mm *Sprenggranate mit Kopfzünder* (high-explosive, with nose fuse) *GrZ Granate-Zünder* (shell) (**2**) was a 2.75kg steel projectile containing 0.16kg of cast TNT (*Füllpulver 02*). It was capped by a grey-painted, mild-steel *Kanone Zünder 1916 mit Verzogerung* (cannon fuse 1916 with delay), which replaced a normal time fuse, as the latter could not easily be set in a moving tank. Increasingly constricted by an Allied naval blockade, German armament manufacturers were forced to substitute lower-quality, less corrosion-resistant aluminium, zinc and steel for bronze or brass components. The round's cartridge case base was painted red, with a black stencilled 'V' (*Verzogerung* – delay).

To provide close-range anti-personnel capabilities, 3.6kg canisters (**3**) packed with 185 16.2g lead balls, backed by a wooden disc, acted like a shotgun when fired. Its thin cylindrical tin shell and overlapping cover served to contain the projectile's internal components, which then burst forth when leaving the barrel. By spring 1918, the large stockpiles of captured 57mm Cockerill-Nordenfelt/Belgian-made École Pyrotechnique (Antwerp) 57mm canister rounds had largely been used up.

The 57mm×222–224mmR (rimmed) brass cartridge case shared by these projectiles included a detonating primer and a TNT (*Rohrpulver* – tube powder – such as RP C/06 or C/12) propelling charge. Stencilling was common on fixed shells, as well as information on the base, so the user would not have to remove the round from a rack to discover its contents. As cases could be reused some half-dozen times with cordite charges (a life of the case figure deduced by the number of firing-pin marks on the base), the expansion produced by each firing meant the base needed to be 'rectified' by turning metal off the lower part to regain the correct dimensions; this process progressively weakened it.

1

2

3

With facilities in Britain at Erith, Kent, and in Stockholm and Spain, Maxim produced the 'legitimate' 6-pounder (57mm) casemate guns until 1897, when the naval shipbuilding and engineering firm, Vickers, acquired his company. Three years later, Vickers, Sons & Maxim resumed production, and in 1892 Russia took the gun into service, alongside the 57mm L/48 coastal version that the Alexandrovsky Steel Works and St Petersburg Ordnance Factory produced under licence. In the East, as part of the fighting around Warsaw in August 1915, German forces – supported by the specialist infantry units that had helped reduce Belgian frontier fortresses and Antwerp the previous year – captured the symbol of Russian rule in Poland, the formidable Nowo-Georgiewsk fortress. As well as accepting the surrender of the 90,000-man garrison, the Germans captured one million shells and hundreds of cannons, including 57mm Maxim models. Used predominantly as replacements for the 6-pounder pieces removed from captured British tanks after mid-1917, they were also used on some A7Vs, including 'Schnuck' (504). Both the Cockerill and the Maxim cannon were installed after armour had been mated to the chassis, as 16 of the 20 A7Vs produced were originally intended to be females.

The *Kampfwagen-Erinnerungsabzeichen* (tank memorial badge) was made from silver, surrounded by a wreath of oak and laurel leaves on the left and right respectively. Instituted on 13 July 1921 by the German Defence Minister, this private-purchase badge was awarded to 99 former tankers who had participated in at least three armoured actions, or had been wounded during such activity. (Public Domain)

As part of the initial run of four male A7Vs the German War Ministry's APK (Artillerie-Prüfungskommission, Artillery Examination Commission) installed a makeshift *Bocklafette* (trestle gun carriage), into vehicles 502/540, 505, 506 and 507. Cannon mounted on such platforms incorporated simple open sights comprising a sliding notch (internal) and bead (external), which necessitated a T-shaped shield cut-out above the barrel. As this opening frequently drew enemy fire, and hampered visibility, the port visor, which was armour-shuttered, offered a substitute. Starting in April 1918 these vehicles received improved *Sockellafette* (pedestal gun carriage) mounts, which were also installed on the remaining A7Vs. Corrupted to 'Socle', this mount had originally been produced by Berlin's Spandau Ordnance Works for use in the British-inspired A7V-U ('U' meaning *Umlaufende Ketten* – circulating tracks). Found suitable for use in the A7V, as well as *Beute* British tanks, the counterbalanced system enabled the gunner to rest on a fixed padded seat and knee cushions, and traverse the gun by shuffling from side to side.

*Sockellafette* cannon were partnered with a sophisticated Goerz-produced 4× RblF 16 (*Rundblick-Fernrohr* – panoramic telescope), with a 10-degree, (177mm) visual field. Initially used vertically with field artillery for direct and indirect targeting, the sight needed to be mounted at 90 degrees to fit within the A7V's mantlet space. This necessitated removing the collimator, as its fixed levelling bubble would not have worked at the new angle, as well as reorienting the reticule and adding a vertical opening in the shield. Being a panoramic sight, the objective lens (nearest the eye) and its light-blocking leather eye cover could remain in a fixed position, while a rectifying prism between it and the ocular (object glass) assembly enabled the latter section to move independently, and in synchronization with the barrel's elevation and depression. As the eyepiece could not be focused, the gunner needed to position his eye about 20mm from the objective lens; because the reticule and target image occupied the same focal plane, the lack of relative motion meant they appeared as a single image. Although the panoramic sight promoted increased accuracy at distance, it was not well liked by A7V gunners, who lobbied unsuccessfully for returning to the simpler open sights that enabled them to maintain visual contact with the target better while their vehicle was moving and during combat.

To coordinate targeting between the gunner and commander, a direction indicator was positioned above the cannon's recoil cylinder, while a series of Zeiss lights over the right-hand vision port indicated the latter's firing control intentions: white (attention), red (fire) and off (load the gun). Following the determination of a target's range, the gunner used a pair of hand-wheels for fine-tuning traverse and elevation. The firing process involved inserting a round into an open breech block, pushing the right-mounted lever forward to seal the chamber, and rotating the empty cartridge case extractor claws back into their cavities. The directing cam subsequently struck the sear to fire the round. Pulling the lever back reversed the process, reopened the breech, and expelled the spent cartridge case. The use of a simple, one-spring firing mechanism made for easy cleaning and assembly, while the combination of sturdy, fixed mounts, recoil-reducing spring and hydraulic buffers minimized breech movement to just 150mm, and kept the gun on the target. When using shot its initial muzzle velocity and maximum range were 487m/s and 6,675m respectively – not that such distances were practical for contemporary tank-on-tank engagements. A shell projectile could be fired out to roughly 2,700m, while canister was effective to just 300m.

Leutnant Albert Müller (with binoculars), and crewmen, of A7V 'Schnuck' (504) during training near Reims in summer 1918. Several crewmen sport an Iron Cross 2nd Class ribbon, and the marksman lanyard (one acorn) worn by one man hints that he is the gunner. (NARA)

# A7V INTERIOR

1. Recoil cylinder
2. Breech block
3. Firing lever
4. *Sockellafette*
5. Gunner's platform
6. Inner traverse wheel
7. Outer elevation wheel
8. Breech plate
9. Armour-shuttered vision slits
10. Goerz 4× panoramic sight
11. Mantlet
12. Front roof louvre
13. Targeting dial
14. Communication lights
15. Rope toggle
16. Loader's seat

## MOBILITY

The A7V relied on a lengthened Holt tractor chassis, very like the French CA1 Schneider and the Saint-Chamond tanks, where its fully tracked Caterpillar suspension comprised running gear supports of six box-section girders that strengthened the framework. A pair of three tie-rod-connected bogie sets of five road wheels and two return rollers were mated with two helicoid suspension springs. Grousers were added to the bogies to help keep the 48 pressed-steel track plates connected to their bolted cast-steel links, all of which were adjusted via a chain tightening gear attached to the front-mounted idler wheel.

Although the A7V was originally intended to house a single 200hp engine, none was available; therefore two 100hp Daimler four-cylinder, water-cooled 165-204 motors were mounted in the vehicle's centre instead. One was modified to run in the opposite direction from the other, and each incorporated an internal exhaust muffler connected to an external venting pipe, or simple opening. The front radiator cooled water from the port engine, while the rear one functioned similarly for its starboard partner. An award-winning, easily accessible Pallas concentric float-type carburettor provided the necessary fuel and air mix which, using an auxiliary nozzle, allowed the mechanism to function regardless of the vehicle's orientation. It also limited the engine's rpm, much like a governor, and along with the manifolds, was positioned along the cooler engine periphery.

A pair of double cone clutches were added for smoother shifting and integrating gears running at different speeds, while a large, complicated, three-speed Adler gearbox controlled each engine's drivetrain. Parallel, single-row final drive assembly shafts extended from this casting to power the rear-mounted drive sprockets. Secondary, pull rod-activated shafts extended rearwards to end in large, external contraction-type steering brake-drums, while two 250l petrol/benzene fuel tanks, one for each engine, sat beneath the deck and slightly forward.

# THE STRATEGIC SITUATION

Following the Miracle on the Marne in September 1914, when British and French forces checked Imperial Germany's war-opening drive on Paris, and the subsequent Race to the Sea in which each side unsuccessfully tried to outflank the other, the Western Front quickly degenerated into an almost impenetrable network of trenches, barbed wire and defensive positions that extended from the English Channel to the Swiss border. In contrast to the Allies' fixation with recapturing north-eastern France, the Germans were largely content to adopt a force-multiplying, active-defensive stance, especially as an attacker would need to manoeuvre large infantry forces across an increasingly devastated landscape, while being subjected to fire from modern machine guns and rapid-firing artillery, as well as poison gas.

As the battles throughout 1915 proved largely inconclusive, British commanders conducted a massive offensive in the Somme sector the following year to break the deadlock, but the resulting casualties compared to ground gained quickly became unsustainable. A German attempt to eliminate the Verdun bulge proved similarly unsuccessful, and with reserves limited, and overseas supplies restricted by an ever-tightening enemy naval blockade, a war of attrition was to be avoided. When the United States abandoned its neutral stance and declared war against Germany on 6 April 1917, Ludendorff and other senior German commanders believed that outright victory was unlikely. In an effort to secure a decisive military victory in the West that would position Imperial Germany for a palatable armistice before the Americans arrived in strength, several successive operations were planned in spring 1918, under the collective name *Kaiserschlacht* (Kaiser's Battle).

Unlike conventional offensives conducted over several days, which softened an enemy's forward positions with artillery to facilitate a follow-on attack by masses of vulnerable infantry, this operation involved German Stosstruppen (shock troops) tactics designed to avoid these high casualty/low gain outcomes. Instead, brief bombardments (often creeping, and mixed with various poison-gas shells) were to disrupt enemy defences and their command and control capabilities, just prior to the arrival of these assault infantry formations. In coordination with other arms, Stosstruppen incorporated specialized weapons, such as flamethrowers, grenades and light machine guns, to maintain a rapid tempo, exploit gaps in enemy defences, and leave the reduction of strong-points to more traditional infantry. With originators like Oskar von Hutier and Max Hoffmann having seen their infiltration concepts successfully applied against Riga (Russia) and Caporetto (Italy) in 1917, and elsewhere, such techniques reached their epitome in 1918.

Both these German *Stosstruppen* wear M1916 Stahlhelms, M1915 button-covering tunics and grenade-filled sandbags, and carry 7.92mm Karabiner Modell 1898 AZs. The man on the left has an M1822 'general service' spade, likely to have a sharpened blade for close-quarter fighting; he wears cloth puttees and M1901 ankle boots. His comrade has two M1907 water bottles, M1887 haversack, M1866 boots, cloth-covered M1915 gas mask and M1911 wire cutters. (NARA)

In contrast to the well-established front lines in the West, the East's vast battle-space did not unduly impede operational manoeuvre. After three years of largely fruitless combat, Russia succumbed to financial and military deficiencies, which combined with political instability to force Russia from the fight, and into a state of civil war. On 11 November 1917, Ludendorff decided to launch a major offensive between Arras and Saint-Quentin, without consulting either the German government or the nominal Chief of the General Staff, Generalfeldmarschall Paul von Hindenburg. Rather than attempt to reach the English Channel to the west, and risk over-extending logistics, the plan involved penetrating the fronts of the British Third and Fifth Army, between Arras and Saint-Quentin, the town that lay near Fifth Army's boundary with the French First Army. From there, the emphasis would shift to the north-west in an ill-defined effort to capture Arras, and corner British forces, in an effort to achieve a favourable armistice. As peace negotiations with Russia began the following month,

German pioneers placing a 20×30×5cm container (filled with 18× 200g explosive blocks (perdite/picric acid)) as part of a wooden box *Flachmine 17*. These anti-tank mines were then covered and concealed with earth, as part of barbed-wire and trench defences, and detonated by one of four spring percussion lighters, or by the victim's weight. (NARA)

military demands facing the Germans in the East were considerably reduced. Able to reallocate some 50 divisions to other sectors such as Italy or the Western Front, German commanders in the West found themselves with a manpower influx that seemed entirely capable of defeating the British. The Germans believed the Allies Powers were exhausted, having undertaking major operations in 1917 at Arras, Messines, Passchendaele and Cambrai; as they possessed a numerical advantage in the West for the first time since 1914, Ludendorff's planned offensive seemed viable.

Although American forces had been arriving in Western Europe since 26 June 1917, the Germans hoped to conclude operations before their new adversary could substantially reinforce the Allied effort. By mid-February 1918, most of the units transfered from Germany's Eastern Front had been integrated in the West. Their Western Front's division count expanded to 177, out of a total of 241 in all. Of these 177 divisions,

A very reliable Albion A10 3-tonne lorry deposits 9-litre tins to the Rollencourt 'Tankdrome', near Cambrai, where Mark IVs are undergoing maintenance and replenishment. The tins are likely painted green, red or khaki, and as none appears to be black, with an 'O' (oil), 'P' (paraffin/kerosene) or 'W' (water), they hold petrol. Due to the necessities of war, water tins had often previously carried fuel. (*Illustrated War News*)

110 were in the front line, with 50 of the 110 allocated to the relatively narrow front for the attack. The British Fifth Army opposite these German forces, depleted by the previous year's fighting, had abandoned the reliance on a well-established, continuous trench-line system. Having experienced the benefits of German defensive tactics and techniques, the Allied Powers increasingly deployed in depth, the better to absorb a sustained attack. By reducing the proportion of conventional forward forces in the outpost zone (also known as the forward zone) in favour of snipers, active patrols and machine-gun positions, the defenders' losses could be minimized. Beyond the range of German field artillery, the battle zone comprised the main resistance line, although the various redoubts were not always mutually supportive, and they were susceptible to enemy infiltration. Farther back, the rear zone included supply dumps, and reserves whose task was counter-attacking or sealing off penetrations. On paper, a British infantry division (since early 1918 with nine infantry battalions, rather than 12) was to deploy three, four and two in each of the respective zones, front to rear. As the British prepared to contest the anticipated German offensive, limited labour and construction resources meant that when the time came, few of the defensive positions were ready, and the second and third lines were almost entirely theoretical.

## OPERATION *MICHAEL*

By early 1918, the British command increasingly suspected that German forces would make a decisive move, but outnumbered by 26 divisions to 63, and ill prepared to resist, they were overwhelmed when Ludendorff's offensive finally erupted from the Hindenburg Line on 21 March. At 0440hrs, the Germans initiated the war's largest artillery barrage to soften enemy front-line positions along a very foggy, 95km front. Five hours later, some 1,100,000 rounds had devastated 400 sq km of the British Third and Fifth Armies' positions. The infantry-heavy, non-motorized offensive, made up of Seventeenth (Otto von Below), Second (Georg von der Marwitz), and Eighteenth Armies (Oskar von Hutier), with the latter supported by Seventh Army's corps-sized Gruppe *Gayl*, made excellent progress. By day's end, the British had suffered nearly 55,000 casualties, and were streaming west. Of the 370 British tanks that were spread out along the line, only 180 saw action, with most breaking down as they withdrew alongside the infantry. Although the older Marks I–III had since been withdrawn from front-line service, in an environment that required rapid movement and force reallocation, the Mark IVs' slow speed proved a considerable handicap as they were frequently subjected to successful German anti-tank elements. As part of the German effort, just south of Saint-Quentin ATD 1's five A7Vs, plus five *Beute* tanks, took the field for the first time under Hauptmann Walter Greiff, in support of 36th (West Prussia) Division.

After two days the British Fifth Army was in full retreat, and the French capital was subjected to long-range shelling from the world's largest artillery piece, Krupp's 'Paris Gun'. On 24 March, the Germans captured Péronne and Bapaume as they pushed inexorably forward, although the newly won territory was difficult to traverse, as much of it consisted of the shell-torn wilderness left by the 1916 battle of the Somme. The French sent reinforcements to the beleaguered sector, which, in the opinion of the British commander-in-chief, Haig, and the British government, were applied too slowly to have an effect. In an effort to coordinate forces, the

French General Ferdinand Foch was appointed commander-in-chief of all Allied forces on the Western Front, but by then the Third Army had disengaged from the retreating Fifth Army to avoid being outflanked. Within five days, the Germans had recaptured all the land they had lost in the Somme sector during the previous 16 months, and were closing on the deserted city of Amiens; if it fell the route to Abbeville, just 15km from the English Channel, would be open.

Ludendorff's lack of a coherent strategy to complement the new infantry assault tactics was illustrated by his statement to his Army Group commander, Rupprecht, Crown Prince of Bavaria, that 'We chop a hole. The rest follows.' Such unenlightened use of specialist formations blunted their potential by attacking strongly entrenched British units at the most important sections along the line, while much of the German advance was squandered on areas of secondary operational importance. As the Germans showed signs of fatigue and found it increasingly difficult to move supplies forward, fresh Australian formations that had been steadily inserted into the battle further hampered German efforts. The following day German units took Noyon, Roye and Chaulnes, as well as Albert and Miraumont north of the River Somme, but the offensive was slowing. On 26 March 1918 the British introduced their new Mark A Whippet tank; operated by a single driver, featuring an engine and transmission that were separate from the crew and using low, weight-reducing tracks, it was a faster, more nimble complement to the heavier Mark IV.

At Arras on 28 March, Ludendorff launched a hastily prepared, ultimately unsuccessful attack (Operation *Mars*) against the British Third Army's right flank, to try to widen the gap between it and Fifth Army. With the great German offensive noticeably waning, Ludendorff called for a final push between the rivers Somme and Avre starting on 30/31 March 1918; a day earlier, on 29 March, the Australian 9th Infantry Brigade (3rd Australian Division) had been repositioned to protect the small manufacturing and farming town of Villers-Bretonneux, just east of Amiens. With British and Australian resistance stiffening, the German point of impact cascaded southwards into

Purpose-built to pierce the more heavily armoured British Mark IV, the German bolt-action Mauser 13.2mm *Tank Abwehr Gewehr*, or 'T-Gewehr', entered combat in February 1918. The tungsten-infused steel round's large size and high velocity (780m/s) produced a fearsome recoil that necessitated both the gunner and ammunition bearer/ spotter being trained in its use, in case one was injured during firing. (Public Domain)

Australian artillerymen load separate lyddite (picric acid)-filled high-explosive shells (single driving band around a yellow round, with a light-green band) into a BL (breech-loading) 9.2in Mk I siege howitzer, as evidenced by the short barrel. Just visible to the right, the piece's collapsible counterweight box has been filled with some 8 tonnes of earth. Note the camouflage net over the distant gun crew and the narrow-gauge railway line that transported the queue of ammunition. (NARA)

**OPPOSITE**

As the initial operation of the German Spring Offensive, *Michael* gained a significant amount of territory, but due to the Germans' lack of motorized transport, stalled after three weeks without having achieved its objectives, resulting in an operational dead end.

the French First Army's left. By the end of March, Australian and New Zealand units had largely relieved British units along most of the stiffening Somme front south of Albert. On 4 April, 15 German divisions, supported by a 1,200-gun bombardment, assaulted just seven Allied divisions in a concerted effort to capture Villers-Bretonneux and threaten Amiens, some 15km to the west. With three Australian brigades in reserve, and the Australian Corps distributed across the River Somme for use in recapturing Villers-Bretonneux should it fall, Fourth Army's commander, General Henry Rawlinson, felt he could hold the area. A gifted yet methodical tactician, Rawlinson's battlefield leadership at Ypres, Neuve Chapelle, Loos and elsewhere paid off as the German attack was halted less than half a kilometre from the town to stabilize a front along the line Moreuil–Marcelcave–Sailly-le-Sec. To the south, 30 French divisions implemented their own advance from south of the River Luce, which deterred German efforts to capture the Cachy plateau and penetrate Rawlinson's right flank, and promoted relative stability in the Villers-Bretonneux sector for the next two weeks.

On 4 April, German military authorities declared the capture of some 90,000 prisoners since the start of Operation *Michael*, and on 5 April Ludendorff formally ended the offensive in favour of initiating Operation *Georgette* four days later in Flanders. As the Germans had failed to secure Amiens and areas north, British forces in the Somme sector maintained contact with their supply centres, stocked from coastal facilities at Le Havre, Dieppe and elsewhere, and were able to regain their strength. The Prime Minister, David Lloyd George, responded by pouring 140,000 reinforcements into France; most were very young because this late in the war the service age had been reduced. Less fortunately for the Germans, the value of the conquered territory was offset by the great loss of their specialist assault infantry, and the winning of a rather valueless, exposed salient that required large amounts of Germany's scarce manpower to maintain.

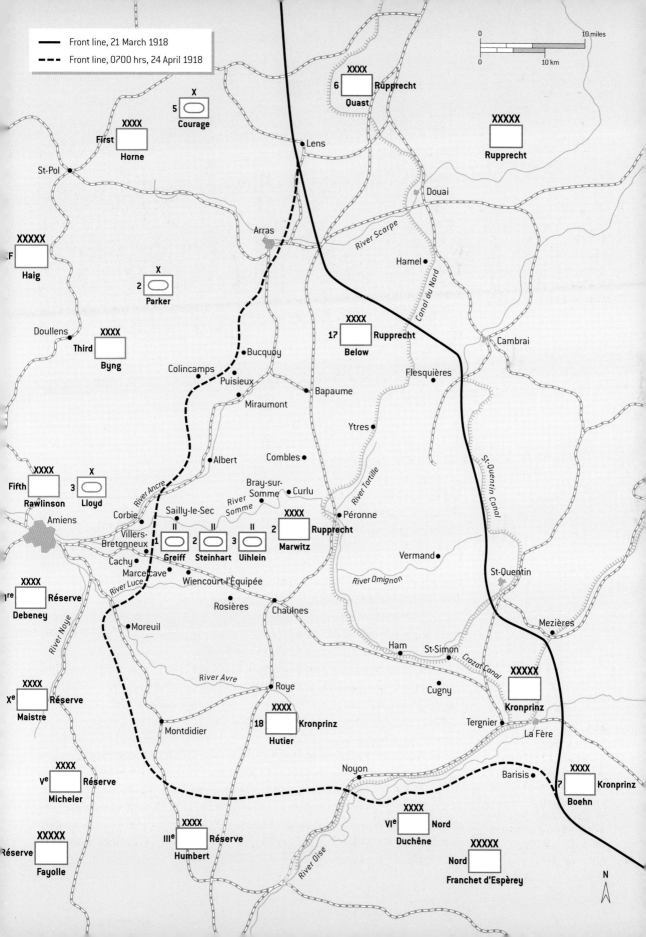

Front line, 21 March 1918

Front line, 0700 hrs, 24 April 1918

0 ___ 10 miles

0 ___ 10 km

X
5 ⬭
Courage

XXXX
First
Horne

6 ▭ Rupprecht
Quast

XXXXX
Rupprecht

St-Pol

Lens

Douai

Arras

River Scarpe

Hamel

Canal du Nord

Cambrai

XXXXX
CF
Haig

X
2 ⬭
Parker

XXXX
17 ▭ Rupprecht
Below

Flesquières

Doullens

XXXX
Third
Byng

Bucquoy

Colincamps

Puisieux

Miraumont

Bapaume

Ytres

River Tortille

St-Quentin Canal

Albert

Combles

XXXX
Fifth
Rawlinson

X
3 ⬭
Lloyd

River Ancre

Bray-sur-
Somme

Curlu

Péronne

Corbie

Sailly-le-Sec

River Somme

XXXX
2 ▭ Rupprecht
Marwitz

Amiens

Villers-
Bretonneux

II
1 ⬭
Greiff

II
2 ⬭
Steinhart

II
3 ⬭
Uihlein

Vermand

St-Quentin

Cachy

Marcelcave

Wiencourt-l'Èquipée

River Omignon

Mezières

XXXX
1re Réserve
Debeney

River Noye

River Luce

Rosières

Chaulnes

Moreuil

Ham

St-Simon

Crozat Canal

Cugny

XXXXX
Kronprinz

XXXX
Xe Réserve
Maistre

River Avre

Roye

Tergnier

La Fère

Montdidier

XXXX
18 ▭ Kronprinz
Hutier

XXXX
Ve Réserve
Micheler

Noyon

Barisis

7 ▭ Kronprinz
Boehn

XXXXX
Réserve
Fayolle

XXXX
IIIe ▭ Réserve
Humbert

River Oise

XXXX
VIe ▭ Nord
Duchêne

XXXXX
Nord
Franchet d'Espèrey

N

# THE COMBATANTS

## BRITISH

### ORGANIZATION

In March 1916 the new British Mark I tanks were first organized as a Heavy Section ('Heavy Branch' after that November) of the Machine Gun Corps under Swinton. Originally stationed at Siberia Farm near Bisley Camp, Surrey, the formation was subsequently moved on 4 June 150km to the north-east, to Elveden Camp. Here six companies were soon raised, four of which (A, B, C and D) were transferred to France on 13 August 1916, where they fought at Flers-Courcelette on 15 September. On 18 November, the increasing availability of tanks meant that companies were organized into three-company battalions, a triangular configuration that promoted flexibility and command manageability. Each was sequentially letter-designated (numbered after January 1918), with sections listed as 1–9 or 1–12. A few months later two-battalion brigades were formed, and on 27 July 1917 the Heavy Branch, Machine Gun Corps, was officially designated as the Tank Corps.

For the next few months, various vehicles-to-unit ratios and configurations were explored in relation to availability, logistics and battlefield experience. In early 1917, battalion tank strength was officially 60 vehicles, but this was reduced to 48 (36 fighting and 12 training machines), and in 1918 reduced again to 42, with just six of these allocated for training. By April, the Tank Corps had expanded to five brigades, with each officially consisting of a headquarters, three battalions, a signal company, a tank supply company and a motorized transport column. Heavy battalions (equipped with

Mark IVs) comprised three companies, divided into four sections (three fighting and one for training/reserve), each of three tanks, while medium (Whippet) battalions were fielded as five sections (four fighting and one for training/reserve), with four tanks each.

## TRAINING

Having established the Armoured Car Section, Motor Machine Gun Corps at Siberia Farm on 16 February 1916, Swinton gathered hand-picked candidates for secret individual and collective crew and manoeuvre training the following month. Tank trainees with motoring, mechanical or technical backgrounds were mostly chosen from 18th, 19th and 21st Royal Fusiliers, and now undertook vehicle operation and maintenance instruction. As actual vehicles were not yet available, they were forced to use canvas mock-ups, and although officer candidates generally had served in France and Gallipoli, many of the lower ranks had little or no front-line experience. Weapons procurement was also limited, with machine guns provided by the Ministry of Munitions. Just up the road at Bullhousen Farm, Royal Navy personnel provided instruction on the 6-pounder cannon, but otherwise the programme was limited to physical training and marching. Soldiers who desired a temporary commission with armoured forces were sent to the Machine Gun Corps Cadet School at nearby Pirbright. As part of their four-and-a-half months of tank training, some 600 cadets were organized into three Officer Training Battalions (11th and 19th at Pirbright and 24th at Hazeley Down, Winchester), and worked through a daily 0630hrs to 2100hrs regime.

As the tank programme expanded, and Mark Is became available for training, Swinton relocated to Elveden, Suffolk, where Canada Farm Camp provided a more

'Tankodrome' near Cambrai, where Mark IVs are grouped in squadrons and divisions, including vehicles displaying serial numbers 528 (foreground), and 2698 (just behind). The area between the sponson and the vehicle's front was reserved for its call sign. Repair workshops, petrol store sheds and ammunition magazines are nearby. (*Illustrated War News*)

The Tank Corps badge was instituted on 28 July 1917, but it was not approved by the sovereign until 11 September that year. It was officially made available to combatants for meritorious service the following January, but a motto was not applied as the unit was not deemed an established force. The version seen here was awarded until 1924; 'Fear Naught' was added to subsequent iterations after suggestions such as 'Dreadnought' and 'Push On' had been considered. (Public Domain)

isolated location, with greater space in which to train across terrain that was soon manipulated to mimic that at the front line. For the next eight weeks, crews learned to drive and fight their vehicles, minus their side sponsons and main armament. The drilling staff comprised warrant officers and NCOs from The Rifle Brigade who possessed combat experience, which later included stints with combat-allocated tank units. Initially, tank instruction was conducted on stationary vehicles, where cadets were trained on basic drive components. During subsequent training in manoeuvres, instructors would often covertly disable a component that the crew would then have to identify, diagnose and fix.

To accommodate the increasing number of British tanks better, in June 1916 the War Office established a new facility at Bovington, Dorset, some 180km south-west of London. The facility, just north of the railway station at Wool, was occupied on 27 October. Junior officers were posted to the tank depot at Wareham, where they received training in revolver shooting and carrier-pigeon use. At Bovington Camp instructors introduced them to the tank's mechanisms and structure in the workshop hangers, where each explained the functions of a particular component. All-arms integration was emphasized, especially between tanks and infantry, with a focus on communications and the use of terrain. Additional studies included military law, administration, first aid, sanitation, bombing, gas, reconnaissance, reading aircraft reconnaissance photos, the Lee-Enfield rifle, the Lewis gun, signalling, night movements and bayonet fighting, plus physical training, compass and topography training – the latter triggering a 'Return to Unit' should the candidate fail. 6-pounder gunnery practice, now with the weapon as part of an attached sponson, was conducted just to the south at Lulworth Camp. In order to simplify the application of training into something of a best practices list, tankers were told, among other things, to remember their orders, to shoot quick and low as it was better to kick up dust than miss, to economize on ammunition by not 'killing' a target more than once, and to watch for friendly infantry and the progress of neighbouring tanks. After passing training in Britain, tankers undertook collective and tactical training in France. Between the factory and the front, No. 20 Squadron members performed mechanical testing at Newbury, Berkshire. From there vehicles were transported by rail to Avonmouth and later Southampton and Richborough, before being shipped to another squadron detachment at Le Havre, France. The tanks were tested again near Bermicourt, and transported by rail to the Plateau railhead near the Central Workshops and 'Tankodrome' at Érin, France. A driving school was also established at a section of evacuated German trench works at nearby Wailly.

## TACTICS

Considering the novelty of the British tank force in 1916, armoured theory was understandably basic, and largely the result of allowing for the vehicles' limited technological and operational capabilities. Swinton's memorandum, *Armoured Machine Gun Destroyers*, provided some direction for how to employ the tank in selecting a weak spot as a point of attack, forcing a penetration and expanding the position to allow supporting forces to move into the vacuum. Many British armour authorities envisaged using the tank in roles that enabled 'penetration with security', as stipulated in 'Training Note No. 16', of February 1917. While traditional cavalry was to continue to perform reconnaissance and screening roles, tanks were to integrate with infantry, and enable them to gain enemy defensive positions (preferably into the enemy artillery), as well as to provide mutual support in which the strengths of one arm could balance the weaknesses of the other. Accompanying assault infantry would stay with an advancing tank, and as they could not hold a captured trench at the same time as continuing to perform their duties, 'moppers up' following on would secure the captured ground. No fewer than two tanks were to operate together, and preferably four.

In a typical application, a 12-tank company would attack with its right and left four-vehicle sections crossing an enemy position to fan out to the sides, while the centre section would be free to push straight ahead. An attack against trenches with an artillery barrage involved three tanks in line at intervals of 100m to 200m, each followed by infantry, with a single tank and additional infantry acting as a reserve. Without an artillery barrage the centre tank would be positioned 150m ahead, and without accompanying infantry, would act as 'artillery' and as a scout. In the field, tank sections would act as mobile strong points, while interspersed infantry files would advance as part of the firing line.

## COMMAND AND CONTROL

To improve command and control in the field, individual tanks were given names (generally by their commanders), which corresponded with each vehicle's position within the battalion hierarchy. Alphabetical designations sequentially mirrored their

### MARK IVs AND WHIPPETS AT VILLERS-BRETONNEUX, 24 APRIL 1918

**'A' Company, 1st Battalion, 3rd Tank Brigade**
(A/Major Herbert G. Pearsall MC)

1st Section (A/Captain John Brown MC):
Male A1 (4086) (2nd Lieutenant Frank Mitchell)
Female (Lieutenant Edward Hawthorn)
Female (Lieutenant J. Webber)

Section of Lieutenant Charles Grove:
Male (Lieutenant Charles Gibbons)
Female (2nd Lieutenant S.C. Bell)

**'X' Company, 3rd Battalion, 3rd Tank Brigade**
(A/Captain Thomas R. Price MC)

8th Section (Lieutenant Lawrence Hore):
'Crustacean III' (A286): Lieutenant Lawrence Hore
(A255): 2nd Lieutenant D.M. Roberts
(A244): 2nd Lieutenant George Ritchie
(A256): 2nd Lieutenant Harry Dale

5th Section (2nd Lieutenant Arthur Elsbury):
'Crossmichael' (A233): 2nd Lieutenant Arthur Elsbury
'Crawick' (A236): 2nd Lieutenant Thomas Oldham
'Centaur III' (A277): Sergeant Charles Parrott

respective battalions, so for example 5th Battalion tanks received names beginning with the letter 'E', in a style similar to the Royal Navy's tradition of naming ships of the same class with the same initial letter. Initial letters were also made part of individualized call-signs and crew numbers, such as 'Eldorado' (E43), 'Explosive' (E7) and 'Eradicator' (E19). In 'A' Battalion (1st Battalion during 1918) tank A1 would be the first of four tanks in the first of three sections in 1st (post 1918 'A') Company. On the Mark IV, call-signs were applied to the vehicle's front side, and if a tank was transferred to another battalion, the call-sign and the name would be changed accordingly. Tanks were also given a permanent, unique four-digit War Department number, placed on the rear side for administrative purposes.

To communicate within the tank, simple coded commands could be banged on the engine cover or transmission, which allowed commanders to express their views to those outside. Hand gestures were similarly effective, such as holding up fingers indicating what gear to use, two fingers directed downward for neutral, and striking the interior once or twice to indicate a desired change of direction to the right or left, respectively. For inter-vehicle signalling, red, green and white discs could be hoisted on a steel pole to produce up to 39 combinations. These codes were also printed on playing cards and distributed to the tankers and supporting infantry. Morse code shutter signals were seldom used as miscommunication was common. For longer distances, runners, observation balloons, Aldis daylight lamps and carrier pigeons could be used, so long as the latter were not employed later than an hour before sunset, as they were liable to roost for the night. Experiments with air–tank communication largely failed, because of the poor visibility within an armoured vehicle, but a telephonic link could connect armour in the field with higher headquarters.

Armies allotted tank brigades or battalions to corps commands. During battlefield commitments, tank brigade commanders were expected to remain at corps headquarters, or at least maintain telephone contact with the corps staff. Tank battalion commanders were to stay with their reserves, or at least be available to regain control of their command once they became disorganized or rallied. Company and section commanders accompanied their units into battle.

## SALVAGE AND REPAIR

Although the question of salvaging damaged or destroyed tanks had been considered early in the development process, the general view was that such efforts were unnecessary for what was perceived as a one-shot asset. Once the vehicles were fielded, however, the resulting losses rekindled the interest in retrieving and repairing existing tanks, thus saving money and resources. Tank salvage started in December 1916 with small repair parties, but as the numbers of British tanks increased over the next year a commensurate increase in salvage and recovery efforts was needed. The volume of spare parts and repair assets required also grew. Every combat-deployed tank company was subsequently allocated a specialist salvage team, which used horses and wagons to extract or salvage disabled vehicles and operated immediately behind their parent unit. Should a vehicle become so severely damaged that it could not be fixed near the front, one of two tank field companies (formerly salvage companies) would transport the vehicle to one of four Central Workshop sections for repairs, while those badly damaged or destroyed were commonly cannibalized. The four

Throughout March 1918 the Royal Flying Corps' No. 62 Squadron flew two-seat Bristol F.2B fighters out of Cachy, Villers-Bretonneux, and Champien (near Roye) in reconnaissance, ground attack, and aerial combat missions; occasionally against Fokker Dr.1s from Manfred von Richthofen's experienced *Jagdgeschwader 1*. The Cachy aerodrome included transportable Bessonneau canvas tents. (Small, Maynard & Co.)

officers and 250 men of 51st Chinese Labour Company were allocated to perform this hazardous work.

Constructed in early January 1917, the facility at Érin, France, some 4km north of the Heavy Branch Headquarters at Bermicourt, came to include workshops, sawmills, a personnel camp, testing ground, an area for railway sidings and a water well yielding several thousand imperial gallons per hour. By 1 April 1917, the workshops consisted of B1 prefabricated aeroplane hangars, assorted shelters, corrugated iron Nissen and canvas Armstrong huts for officers and a dining hall. Seven months later, building started on new workshops at Teneur, which could repair 1,000 tanks within nine somewhat larger B1 hangars. The reorganization of the Tank Corps' technical branch in early January 1918 saw the abandonment of the battalion workshops in favour of a four-section Central Workshop, a Central Stores, five advanced workshops and two tank field companies for salvage work.

On 29 March 1918, the works at Érin moved to Teneur, while those at the former were taken over by the Central Stores, and became a separate entity. A Works Office was also created to streamline repair by defining and allocating man-hours to accomplish each job. It was estimated that on average it took 120 man-hours to repair a tank, with workshop personnel working continuously in eight-hour shifts. Refurbished vehicles were then placed with Advanced Stores for allocation to operational tank units.

## CREWS

British tankers came from a variety of regiments, which resulted in minimal conformity with regard to cap badges and uniforms. HBMGC crews were often drawn from the Motor Machine Gun units, with drivers from the Army Service Corps, as it offered a logistics background. For protection from hot engines, sharp mechanical components and spalling, crews wore leather jerkins and trousers over their uniforms, as well as gloves and boots. Helmets were advisable, as were partially veiled chainmail masks, although the latter were uncomfortable and seldom used.

Engine noise was considerable, and shifting gears required some effort. The large crank handle could be manipulated by up to four crewmen but jerked dangerously during a backfire, while those in the rear risked injury from several hot pipes, engine

# 2ND LIEUTENANT FRANK MITCHELL

Francis 'Frank' Mitchell was born in St Peter Port, on Guernsey in the Channel Islands, on 16 November 1894. Having volunteered soon after the beginning of World War I in September 1914, he served with 'Kitchener's Mob', so named for the clamorous service calls for joining the New Army. Having started as a private in 6th (City of London) Battalion, The London Regiment (City of London Rifles), he also served with the Labour Corps, 18th (County of London) Battalion, The London Regiment (London Irish Rifles), and 15th (County of London) Battalion, The London Regiment (Civil Service Rifles). Between July 1915 and February 1917 he served with the maintenance and repair of armaments and munitions, and as a driver, with the Army Ordnance Corps, attached to 21st Division.

By March 1917, Mitchell was serving as a 2nd lieutenant in the Tank Corps' 1st Battalion. Throughout July and August, he trained for Operation *Hush*, the planned amphibious landing on the Belgian coast, and was also part of 315th Company, Royal Defence Corps. In early 1918 he participated in the British retreat before the German Spring Offensive, and subsequently fought at Second Villers-Bretonneux in April, and east of Amiens in August.

Having earned the Military Cross (awarded for gallantry or meritorious service) for his efforts along the Cachy Switch, Mitchell was further awarded the British War and Victory Medals. After being discharged on 6 November 1918 he worked as a bank clerk.

2nd Lieutenant Frank Mitchell, commander of Mark IV (male) 4086. (Public Domain)

covers and other hazards during movement. Even though fighting inside a tank was exhausting, dangerous work, most British tankers felt it was preferable to acting as infantry, and consequently, there was never a shortage of armour-crew candidates. An engine silencer, six electric lights and better ventilation helped extract the petrol, grease and oil fumes, and improved crew conditions. After operation, which involved high fuel consumption, each tank needed to have grease injected into various track and roller components, generally through specially located apertures.

# GERMAN

## ORGANIZATION

Having agreed to Chefkraft's (Chief of Motor Transport) demand for a defined A7V TO/E, on 29 September 1917 the War Ministry established two Sturm-Panzerkraftwagen-Abteilungen (essentially assault armoured motor vehicle (tank) detachments, or ATDs). A third unit was formed on 6 November, while a fourth was envisaged as a reserve, although in practice its vehicles were used as

# LEUTNANT WILHELM EUGENE BILTZ

Born on 8 March 1877 in Berlin, Wilhelm Biltz graduated from that city's Royal Grammar School in 1895. Having developed an interest in chemistry, he subsequently studied at the Frederick William University, the University of Heidelberg, and from 1898 at the University of Greifswald where he earned a doctorate in natural science (organic compounds). In 1900 Biltz undertook a three-year stint as an assistant, for which he was promoted to an associate professor at the University of Göttingen, specializing in inorganic compounds and colloids, and later moving to analytical and inorganic chemistry and metallurgy. Starting on 15 March 1905 he began lecturing as a full professor at the Clausthal University of Technology, a post he held when war broke out nine years later.

Considering Biltz's scientific background (and age), he was made a Leutnant, served for the war's duration, and earned the Iron Cross 1st Class. He also commanded the German A7V 'Nixe' (561) at the Second Battle of Villers-Bretonneux in 1918. After the war he returned to lecturing for three years before accepting a position as professor and director of the Inorganic-Chemical Institute at the University of Hanover. Noted as the editor of the *Journal of Inorganic and General Chemistry*, Biltz's declining health forced his eventual retirement. Biltz remained single and childless, and died on 13 November 1943 in Heidelberg, Germany.

Leutnant Wilhelm Biltz, commander of A7V 'Nixe' (561), in civilian dress. Although there was no dedicated German tank uniform, on 29 September 1917 the War Ministry required members of this arm to wear the uniform of the *Kraftfahrtruppen*, which included the Prussian guard lace collar *Litzen* to indicate an elite status. As many tankers were understandably loath to trade their *Frontsoldat* uniforms for those of rear-area transport personnel, those from the infantry and artillery were respectively outfitted with uniforms from 1st Guards Foot Regiment and 1st Guards Field Artillery Regiment respectively, although these were rarely worn in case the crewman were captured and suffered harsh treatment. More often, German tankers simply wore leather jackets or jerkins over their standard *Feldgrau* uniforms. Officers were permitted to wear the uniforms of their former regiments. Drivers and mechanics tended to wear standard transport or motor corps uniforms, as they had with their former branch. (Public Domain)

replacements. Reflecting the British pattern each detachment (including ATDs 11–16, equipped with *Beute* tanks) theoretically comprised one male and four female tanks, although in practice A7Vs were almost entirely the former. Instead of creating a separate entity, Chefkraft short-sightedly decided to make the ATDs part of the rear-echelon motor transport branch.

A full-strength ATD (whether equipped with A7Vs or *Beute* tanks) was commanded by a captain, often from inside one of the tanks, with each of the remaining vehicles under a Leutnant, or even an NCO should circumstances warrant it. ATDs 1, 2 and 3 had a complement of 170 personnel, including 81 drivers, 48 machine-gunners, shells were to be employed as needed to further mask the tank's position or movement. Detachment commanders were to have previously overseen a detailed terrain reconnaissance, and briefed their subordinate tank commanders on the findings. In practice, A7Vs tended to be used in mopping-up operations because of the lack of effective contemporary command and control capabilities. Integration with infantry was often lacking, and in some instances discouraged, as evidenced by an OHL extract emphasizing, 'The infantry and tanks will advance independently of one another …', and for the infantry to remain at least 160m away from the tanks to avoid incoming artillery fire.

## COMMAND AND CONTROL

Because of the very limited numbers of tanks produced or captured, ATDs were subordinated to OHL, which parcelled them out to army commands for combat action. Although early on, centralized operational planning and execution proved necessary to control large, conventional infantry forces effectively, the increasing use of specialist Stosstruppen meant the opposite increasingly tended to be true. To maximise the effectiveness of small, very motivated clusters of fast-moving assault infantry, *Auftragstaktik* provided greater flexibility. Instead of orders, these mission-oriented guidelines imparted a commander's intent, which his trained subordinates on the spot then implemented as they saw fit. Considering the rudimentary communications of the period, this mentality promoted rapid reactions to constantly changing battlefield situations. In concert with the concept of *Vollmacht*, in which an authority – usually delegated to a staff officer – could reposition units without prior approval by his direct commanders, this added to the Germans' swift decision-making and implementation process. The German Army

### A7Vs AT VILLERS-BRETONNEUX, 24 APRIL 1918*

Commander: Hauptmann Walter Greiff

**Group I (Oberleutnant Hans von Skopnik, ATD 1)**
Supporting 228th Infantry Division:
'Alter Fritz' (526): Oberleutnant Hans von Skopnik (ATD 1)
'Lotti' (527): Leutnant Paul Vietze (ATD 1)
Unnamed (560): Leutnant Ernst Volckheim (ATD 1)

**Group II (Oberleutnant Otto Uihlein, ATD 3)**
Supporting 4th Guards Infantry Division:
'Gretchen' (501): Leutnant Lappe (ATD 3)
'Baden I' (505): Leutnant Hennecke (ATD 3)
'Mephisto' (506): Leutnant Heinz G. Theunissen (ATD 3)
'Cyklop' (507): Leutnant Bürmann (ATD 3)
Unnamed (541): Leutnant Block (ATD 1)
Unnamed (562): Leutnant Wolfgang Bartens (ATD 1)

**Group III (Oberleutnant Hans Steinhardt, ATD 2)**
Supporting 419th Infantry Regiment (77th Reserve Division):
(II) 'Siegfried' (525): Leutnant Friedrich-Wilhelm Bitter (ATD 2)
(V) 'Nixe' (561): Leutnant Wilhelm Biltz (ATD 2)

Supporting 257th Reserve Infantry Regiment
(77th Reserve Division):
'Schnuck' (504): Leutnant Albert Müller (ATD 2)
(III) 'Elfriede' (542): Leutnant Stein (ATD 2)

*ATD 3's 'Heiland' (540) and ATD 2's (IV) 'Hagen' (543) did not participate owing to mechanical issues.

Four A7Vs during exercises with assault infantry, possibly from 3rd Jäger Assault Battalion, during early summer 1918 at the *Geländefahrschule* (cross-country driving school) in Beuveille, France. (NARA)

also practised a policy in which function overrode standing, and officers were routinely appointed to positions above their actual rank.

Communication between the front lines and higher commands was based on carrier pigeons, dogs and runners, the latter often drawn from crew members. Vehicle to vehicle or vehicle to infantry signalling was conducted using daytime lights, flares or coloured discs. The Germans abandoned signalling flags early on, and wireless remained experimental. Inside the A7V, the dark, noisy interior prevented verbal commands, and the commander was often too occupied with operating his vehicle and negotiating obstacles to assist in target allocation. Hand gestures were frequently the best way to communicate within a buttoned-up tank.

## CREWS

German tank crews were officially a volunteer force, whose members had originated from a variety of army combat and logistics formations. Officers, drivers and mechanics tended to come from *Kraftfahrtruppen* (motor transport troops), while gunners and loaders came from the artillery and machine-gunners from the infantry. All served time with 1st Motor Transport Replacement Section (part of Berlin's pre-war Guards Corps). Focused toward motor vehicle training, the unit included an administration staff, replacement training company, recruit depot and driving school. In addition to the normal 18-man crew, the A7V's design as something of an infantry fighting vehicle meant it accommodated up to eight additional assault infantrymen. As it was for their British and French counterparts, crew comfort was a low priority, with performance hindered by cramped conditions, engine noise, darkness, temperatures up to 50°C, fumes from fuel and oil, and gas: carbon monoxide and nitric oxide produced by cordite. To escape such problems, German tankers frequently rode on the A7V's roof, or walked alongside, during movement in quiet sectors.

# COMBAT

Although the Germans had conquered some 1,930 square km of territory during Operation *Michael*, dwindling reserves of manpower, ammunition and horses sapped endurance, and prompted Ludendorff to call a halt on 5 April 1918. Although the gains were considerable, and included many important towns which the British had paid a high price to secure in 1916 during the Somme fighting, Amiens and Arras remained in British hands. Although other German offensives were soon to be unleashed to the north and south, as soon as effective logistics were re-established in the centre a renewed German effort would be made to take Villers-Bretonneux. Once it and the plateau to

The view southwards between the Bois l'Abbé (right), and the Bois d'Aquenne (left). This former path (now the D523) marked the furthest German penetration west of Villers-Bretonneux on 24 April 1918. (Author)

the west were secured, additional artillery could be brought against Amiens; German Gotha bombers and long-range fire had already forced the Allies to use the city's railway network only at night.

On 11 April General of Cavalry Georg von der Marwitz was given the task of using his Second Army for the offensive slated three days hence. As resources were being brought forward, he repositioned XI and XIV Army Corps between the Avre and Ancre rivers, and consolidated I Army Corps' exposed position to the south. The previous month's hard fighting had taken a toll on his 17 infantry divisions, with only six now considered capable of participating in the attack. Spearheaded by three ATDs, and supported by some 710 aircraft, 1,208 guns and many hundreds of mortars, however, the limited goal of these formations seemed attainable.

Five days later, on 16 April, Lieutenant General Richard Butler, General Officer Commanding British III Corps, ordered Major General Talbot Hobbs (5th Australian Division) to prepare to retake Villers-Bretonneux lest it fall to what was anticipated to be an imminent German attack – although the British expected the attack to be on a much larger scale than the one that actually occurred. With local Allied forces still reorganizing from the previous week's fight for the town, an ad hoc defence by mostly green teenage soldiers of several national forces would have to suffice. As evidence of the latter, just west of Villers-Bretonneux a mix of French, Australian, Moroccan and British infantry crowded within the Bois l'Abbé alongside artillery and cavalry. Several Mark IVs, Mark A Whippets and single-turret French Renault FTs were also present, and constituted a scratch armoured force that grew in number as recently arrived or repaired tanks were rotated back to the field. Three elements of 3rd Tank Brigade, headquartered at Molliens-au-Bois, north-east of Amiens, were involved – 3rd Battalion (Toutencourt), 9th Battalion (Merlimont), and 1st Battalion (Fréchencourt).

Between 0400hrs and 0700hrs the following morning, the Germans initiated an intense gas and conventional barrage to soften up Rawlinson's Fifth Army (Rawlinson had taken over on 4 April) as it defended the area between Albert and the French boundary south of Cachy. Having been attacked earlier in the month, Villers-Bretonneux was now part of the front line after more than three years of relative isolation. Of the 20,000 deadly chemical rounds dropped, 60 per cent fell in and around the town and the Bois l'Abbé, including chlorodiphenylarsine and phosgene (the canisters were marked with a green cross), which targeted eyes, skin, and the respiratory system, as well as mustard gas (marked with a yellow cross) that induced internal and external blistering, nausea and temporary blindness. In the wake of heavy casualties, those that could be withdrawn from the area were stripped and washed at the nearest Regimental Aid Post, where affected skin was dusted with neutralizing sodium bicarbonate.

A Rheinmetall 77mm L/27 1914 gun mated to an Ehrhardt Model 1911 truck in a mobile anti-aircraft artillery role (before 31 May 1916 such combinations were designated as anti-balloon). The spotter is using a Zeiss *Entfernungsmesser* 14 ('rangefinder 1914'), with a missing end cap. Note the soldiers' mix of puttees and boots, and the right-hand soldier setting fuses. (NARA)

Spearheaded by the war's largest A7V concentration (13 vehicles), the German 228th Infantry, 4th Guards and 77th Reserve Divisions attempted to secure the high ground southwest of Villers-Bretonneux, and threaten Amiens. Although the Germans overran much of the area on 24 April 1918, that night saw counter-attacking Australian reinforcements erase most of the Germans' gains.

View of pre-war, undamaged Villers-Bretonneux from directly over the Saint-Quentin–Amiens railway looking north-east, with Corbie just out of sight to the upper left. St John the Baptist's church is visible in the centre right, just up from where A7V 'Alter Fritz' (526) advanced along the Rue d'Herville (horizontal through the main intersection) early in the battle. (Courtesy of the State of Victoria (Department of Education and Early Childhood Development))

Severe cases were taken to better-equipped field ambulances, mobile medical units that were allocated one per brigade. Had the British constructed more dummy trenches, something they were often wont to do, much of the bombardment might have been distributed and wasted. Instead, many of the defending units needed to be rotated into reserve, while the saturated ground was treated with chloride or lime, to little effect.

Bavarian engineer Hauptmann Friedrich Bornschlegel took command of ATD 1, and the untested ATDs 2 and 3, on 18 April, and between the 19th and 21st the three detachments were sent by rail 170km from Charleroi in Belgium to Guillaucourt, France, some 8km east of Villers-Bretonneux. As 'Heiland' (540) had broken down prior to entraining, Bornschlegel's deputy, Hauptmann Walter Greiff, set about the battlefield deployment of the remaining 14 A7Vs. As they detrained, Allied aircraft strafed the group, but having done no damage, and seemingly unaware of the significance of their target, moved on. The A7Vs then moved to Wiencourt-l'Équipée, and their respective *Angriffsbereitstellungen* (assembly positions), although 'Hagen' (543) suffered a cracked cylinder head and remained at Guillaucourt. To avoid enemy artillery fire and aerial detection, ATD 1 remained under a grove of trees 1km north-east of Marcelcave while ATD 2 moved to the nearby sugar factory and ATD 3 headed for the south-eastern edge of the uncultivated Bois d'Hangard. Weeks of winter weather had left the surrounding terrain firm and generally suited for armour employment and, making use of the attack postponements, Greiff focused on getting his tanks up to operational trim.

On 23 April, the area west of Villers-Bretonneux was subjected to yet another heavy gas and artillery bombardment. Combined with intelligence gleaned from the interrogation of recently captured German prisoners, and increased aerial activity that included the elite fighter wing *Jagdgeschwader* 1 – whose noted commander, Manfred von Richthofen, had just been killed over nearby Corbie – the long-anticipated German attack had seemingly arrived. Under a nearly full moon that was occasionally obscured by potential storm clouds, the British tankers of 1st Section, 'A' Company, 1st Battalion were fatigued by having to wear their masks throughout the day as they endured the barrage within the Bois l'Abbé. Their Mark IVs, a 'bull' (male) and two 'bitches' (females), were further hidden from German aerial reconnaissance, having been covered by green and brown-dyed camouflage netting with its leaf-like tags. Around midnight, two low-flying German planes dropped Very lights directly overhead, which illuminated the area in a pale shimmering light as the flares drifted earthward. While the infantry could simply remain still to best avoid detection, the tankers' large vehicles were clearly visible against a dark background. Fearing his section had been discovered, Captain John Brown waited an hour for sufficient cloud cover to move the noisy vehicles out of the woods to a spot some 100m to the east.

With XIV and XI Army Corps attacking south of the River Somme, respectively targeting Villers-Bretonneux and the Bois d'Aquenne, and Cachy to the south, Greiff

VILLERS-BRETONNEUX avant sa destruction · Vue générale

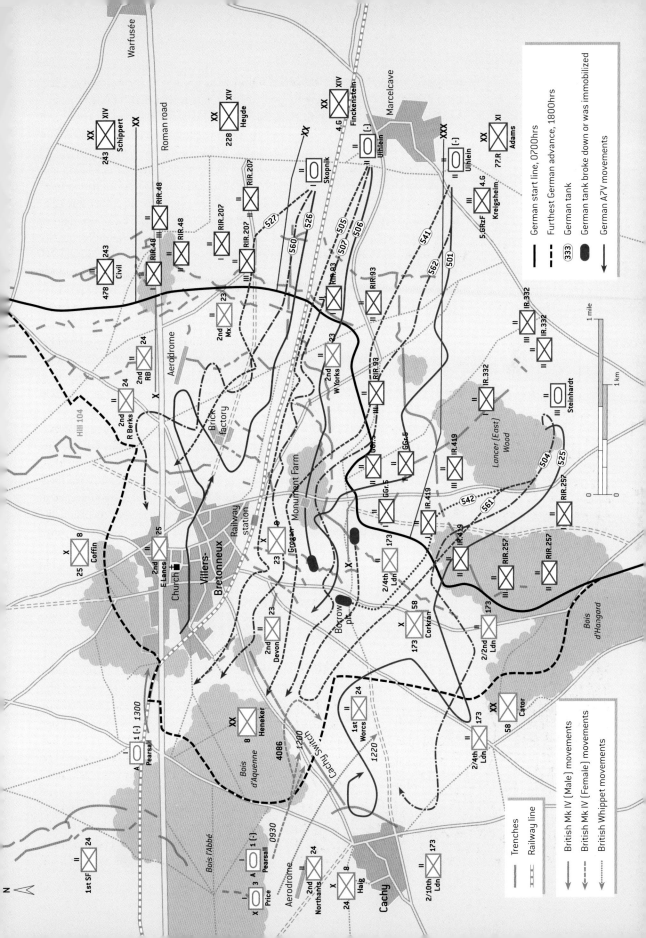

N

Warfusée

Roman road

XX XIV
243 Schippert

XX XIV
228 Heyde

XX XIV
4.G Finckenstein

Marcelcave

XXX XI
77.R Adams

II RIR.48
243

II 243 Civil
478

II RIR.48
III RIR.48

II RIR.207
III RIR.207

II RIR.207
III RIR.207

II Skopnik

II Uhlein [-]

II [-] Uhlein

III 4.G Kriegsheim
5.6RzF

527
526
560
505
507
506

541
562
501

Aerodrome

II 23
2nd Mx

II RIR.93
III

II RIR.93
III

II IR.332
III

II IR.332
III

X 24 2nd RB

II 24
2nd R Berks

Brick factory

II 23
2nd W Yorks

Hill 104

Monument Farm

II GGr.5
III

GGr.5

IR.419

Lancer (East) Wood

II IR.419
III

II IR.332
III Steinhardt

II 25
E Lancs

Railway station

II 23

II 23
Grogan

II GGr.5

II IR.419
III

504
525

X 8 Coffin
25

Church

Villers-Bretonneux

Borrow pit

173

542
561

II IR.419
III

II RIR.257
III

II RIR.257
III RIR.257

II 23
2nd Devon

X 2/4th Ldn

58 Corkran

X 173
2/2nd Ldn

1300

XX 8 Heneker

4086

1200

Cathy Switch

II 24
1st Worcs

1220

II 173
2/4th Ldn

XX 58 Cator

A 1 [-] Pearsall
Pearsall

Bois d'Aquenne

II 24
1st SF

Bois l'Abbé

0930

A 1 [-] Price
Pearsall

Aerodrome

II 24
2nd Northants

X 24 8 Haig

Cachy

173
2/10th Ldn

Bois d'Hangard

1 mile

1 km

German start line, 0700hrs
Furthest German advance, 1800hrs
German tank
German tank broke down or was immobilized
German A7V movements

333

Trenches
Railway line

British Mk IV (Male) movements
British Mk IV (Female) movements
British Whippet movements

organized his A7Vs into three infantry-supporting groups. In the north, Group I's three tanks from ATD 1 were to lead 228th Infantry Division's Brandenburgers, recently depleted in heavy fighting at Hamel, against Villers-Bretonneux, and following the town's capture help secure its northern approaches before returning to Wiencourt-l'Équipée. Group II, comprised of ATD 3 and the rest of ATD 1, was to support the crack Prussian 4th Guards Infantry Division, which intended to push past Villers-Bretonneux, and into the Bois d'Aquenne. Group III's ATD 2's southern approach was to simply lead the lower-quality 77th Reserve Division. This formation, having recently arrived from a lengthy deployment on the Russian Front, and having had a mere five-day briefing by 3rd Jäger Assault Battalion to prepare them for fighting in the west, was to pass the northern edge of the Bois d'Hangard and attack Cachy, before stopping.

As the German tanks moved to their *Ausgangsstellungen* (initial positions) in time for the pre-emptive bombardment slated for early the next morning, each group commander sent the first of their regularly expected written status notifications to the reporting office at the Marcelcave sugar factory. From there a motorcycle squad had the task of forwarding communications to Greiff, who as field commander of the three ATDs was located nearby at 4th Guards Infantry Division's headquarters at Bayonvillers, just east of Warfusée. With one fuel and one ammunition lorry assigned to each ATD once in action, each was to coordinate such deliveries from Guillaucourt independently.

Under the skilled tactical leadership of Major-General (substantive) William Heneker, the defending British 8th Division's sector protecting Villers-Bretonneux included 25th Brigade north of the Roman road, with its 2nd Rifle Brigade forward, 2nd Royal Berkshire in support, and 2nd East Lancashire garrisoning the town. To its right, 23rd Brigade's 2nd Middlesex and 2nd West Yorkshire occupied front-line positions, with 2nd Devonshire behind along the Cachy Switch and the gully south of the town. 173rd Brigade held a sector to Bois d'Hangard, while 174th Brigade idled further west near Cachy and its aerodrome, recently abandoned by the Royal Flying Corps' No. 62 Squadron.

# SECOND VILLERS-BRETONNEUX

At 0445hrs (0345hrs British time) on Wednesday 24 April, German artillery commenced its heaviest bombardment of the week between Hill 104 and the Bois d'Sénécat, some 10km south-west of the Bois d'Hangard. It included various-sized conventional rounds, gas and later, smoke. After targeting British artillery positions for half an hour, the Germans adjusted their fire to hit the town for 15 minutes, before returning to a further 30 minutes of battery-suppression fire. The beleaguered defenders once again donned gas masks, and vacated low-lying and heavily forested areas to avoid the worst effects of the oily, brownish-yellow mustard agent, not to mention falling trees. Visibility, already limited by smoke and gas, was further reduced to only 30m as the warm air surrounding the nearby River Somme had mixed with air over the cold ground to produce an exceptionally thick fog. Throughout the two-hour barrage, French and British artillerymen feverishly responded as best they could.

Some five minutes after dawn Group I's 'heavy field kitchens' initiated the general attack as they advanced through 228th Infantry Division's forward positions at 0650hrs, en route to Villers-Bretonneux. Ten minutes later, the unit's A7Vs 'Lotti' (527), 'Alter Fritz' (526) and the unnamed 560 passed into no-man's-land ahead of III Battalion, 207th Reserve Infantry Regiment. Masked by the lingering fog and smoke, Oberleutnant Hans von Skopnik led the trio generally parallel to the Saint-Quentin–Amiens railway to help maintain bearings. For nearly a quarter of an hour the German tanks ran roughshod over the British infantrymen of 2nd Middlesex before the tankers realized they had outpaced friendly assault infantry. As 48th and 207th Reserve Infantry Regiments remained occupied with clearing the first enemy trench-line, once the A7Vs had repulsed British infantry reserves that emerged from Villers-Bretonneux, Leutnant Ernst Volckheim (560) and Leutnant Paul Vietze (527) turned back to eliminate additional machine-gun nests to get the attack moving. As the *Feldgrau* vehicles, overpainted with blotches of pale green and reddish-brown (plus some clay-yellow on 560) moved eastward, Skopnik continued towards the town alone. Supported by I Battalion, 93rd Reserve Infantry Regiment, the infantry/armour force sowed confusion among the faltering 2nd Middlesex and 2nd West Yorkshire defenders. To the south, Group II and Group III made similar progress against ineffectual small-arms and machine-gun fire.

By 0750hrs the German offensive had made enemy positions east of Villers-Bretonneux untenable. Already, large numbers of British soldiers had been captured, while walking wounded and stragglers were leaving their forward positions, unable to counter the Germans' combination of artillery, assault infantry and armour. In the town, 2nd East Lancashire scrambled to counter the onrushing threat, when Skopnik's lone all-*Feldgrau* A7V rumbled passed St John the Baptist's Church, and drove west through the centre of town along the Rue d'Herville. Stunned defenders skirmished with the behemoth, with its grinning white skull painted on the bow, but inflicted little damage as its commander continued ahead, believing friendly infantry had kept pace. On reaching the town's far side, however, Skopnik realized his error. Vulnerable in such a confined environment, and without supporting infantry, he wisely returned the way he had come.

ATD 2 A7Vs 'Wotan' (563), 'Hagen' (528), 'Siegfried' (525) and 'Schnuck' (504), with their crews during training near Reims in summer 1918. (NARA)

A coloured postcard depicting the farm just south of Villers-Bretonneux where a monument had been erected to remember those who died on 27 November 1870, during the Franco-Prussian War battle nearby. (C. Moncomble)

As Volckheim and Vietze straddled and crisscrossed the British forward positions they had recently overrun, 207th Reserve Infantry Regiment was finally able to comb out the troublesome trenches with grenades and flamethrowers, and move forward. With little reason to continue, isolated pockets of British infantry increasingly surrendered in up to company-sized groups. By 0820hrs, elements of 2nd Middlesex were offering the only organized resistance from the apparent safety of a heavily fortified brick factory at Villers-Bretonneux's eastern edge. Notified by messenger of the situation, Volckheim and Vietze – the latter's A7V sporting a large '527' on its side – moved to engage as Skopnik emerged from his urban excursion. With Group I soon surrounding the fortified British position, Volckheim unleashed devastating 57mm canister and machine-gun fire into the defenders' midst. Vietze soon followed suit from the opposite direction to produce a crossfire that cut down anyone attempting to escape the tank perimeter. After some 20 minutes of carnage, the British defenders began to surrender, and a ceasefire was called. Nearby, elements of 48th Reserve Infantry Regiment conducted house-to-house fighting in the town's northern outskirts, after having pushed 2nd Royal Berkshire out of the nearby aerodrome by 0830hrs.

At the gas-soaked south-western edge of the Bois d'Aquenne, the British 23rd Brigade commander, Brigadier General George Grogan, attempted to ascertain the unfolding situation to his east, but thick fog and smoke continued to obscure the battlefield and muffle sound. Unsure of how best to respond, he ordered Brown's nearby 1st Section tanks to reinforce 1st Worcestershire's positions along the Cachy Switch, stressing that should the Germans overrun the line of discontinuous trenches the high ground within sight of Amiens would give way as well. As the tankers stumbled through gas and

# MARK IV (MALE) GUNSIGHT

Mark IV (male) gunners used fixed sighting scopes that provided 4× magnification. Aiming comprised a simple crosshair reticle, so targeting proved difficult even when stationary as the cannon (which could be manually manoeuvred for fine adjustments) would not remain exactly in place following firing.

undergrowth to reach their waiting 'busses', several succumbed to the fumes, and one was injured when the manual starting crank he was operating suddenly jerked. Although understrength in terms of crew members, the three Mark IVs were soon decamouflaged, and set off to help stem the German onslaught.

Resistance at the brick factory had ended by 0845hrs, and German infantry were still moving into the area. Some of the A7V crewmen dismounted to round up prisoners, amounting to six officers and 160 men (out of an original 20 and 600). Making use of the pause, the three tank commanders met briefly with newly arriving infantry officers, and agreed that Skopnik and Vietze would support 207th Reserve Infantry Regiment into Villers-Bretonneux, while Volckheim would assist 48th Reserve Infantry Regiment to the north of the town. By 0845hrs visibility was improving as the fog thinned, which assisted with Group I's coordination, but it also aided the British. After helping set fire to the aerodrome's hangers, Volckhcim skirted the town's northern edge where he encountered at least three British field guns that engaged him with essentially ineffectual shrapnel at a range of some 300m. Concerned the gunners might switch to solid shot, Volckheim manoeuvred 560 so that outlying structures would offer cover.

Group III had initiated its attack at 0640hrs; a little over three hours later Leutnant Stein's *Feldgrau* 'Elfriede' (542), and Leutnant Albert Müller's 'Schnuck' (504) had advanced from the Bois d'Hangard in support of 257th Reserve Infantry Regiment, which had been slowed by the forest and was not immediately available. Undeterred, the pair went on to eliminate several British machine-gun nests and entrenchments with point-blank enfilading fire, prompting scores of British infantry to surrender. On entering the foggy, open farmland north of the woods, Müller pushed for Cachy as planned, but his partner became disoriented, ventured too far to the north-west, and ran into a sand-and-gravel borrow pit before overturning. Nearby, elements from

## A7V GUNSIGHT

In concert with using traverse and elevation hand-wheels for the QF 57mm Cockerill-Nordenfelt cannon, A7V gunners aligned the tip of the fixed-focus RblF 16 panoramic sight's inverted 'V' reticle with the target. What had been the sight's rotating azimuth scale now applied to elevation, as the piece had been vehicle-mounted sideways, while subsequent, post-firing adjustments would help fine-tune aiming. The Maxim-Nordenfelt's simpler open sight was suited to shorter-range engagements, as an elevated barrel would obstruct visibility for a gunner's direct sighting with the notch and bead.

2nd West Yorkshire, which had been conducting a fighting withdrawal, and were on the verge of giving up, now tried to recover the German vehicle as its 22 crewmen and mounted assault infantry extracted themselves. In the subsequent fight, Stein was killed, but with the tankers outnumbered, and their British adversaries considerably weakened, both parties withdrew. Abandoned but serviceable, 'Elfriede' (542) was not recovered until 15 May 1918, when the French 37th Division overran the area, and with help from two tanks from 1st Battalion, Tank Corps, extracted the first A7V captured by the Allied Powers.

As the uncultivated area around the Bois d'Hangard presented too daunting a tank obstacle, Group III skirted the northern edge of the enemy-occupied wood to gain the open countryside beyond, and in doing so left 77th Reserve Division's left flank hanging and unsecured. Müller continued toward Cachy in support of 419th Infantry Regiment's flank southeast of the village, where he coordinated with the group's remaining A7Vs, Leutnant Friedrich-Wilhelm Bitter's 'Siegfried' (525) and Leutnant Wilhelm Biltz's 'Nixe' (561).

To the north-east, ATD 1's remaining A7Vs, Leutnant Block's 541, and Leutnant Wolfgang Bartens' 562 (both unnamed, but each displaying the detachment's characteristic smiling white skull), advanced to help suppress a knot of enemy resistance just south of Villers-Bretonneux's railway station. Monument Farm – aka 'Kapellengut', chapel property/farm (named after a memorial commemorating soldiers who fell nearby in a battle on 27 November 1870 during the Franco-Prussian War), comprised a hedge-enclosed compound, walls, outbuildings, and a copse of well-maintained trees bordering it on the east and west – an ideal location from which most of 2nd West Yorkshire could make a stand. Leutnant Lappe's 'Gretchen' (501) moved up from the south in support; although the Feldgrau-painted vehicle, with a reddish-brown lower section, did not have a main gun. There had been no time to install it before departing from Charleroi, but its eight machine guns proved devastating against infantry.

Block had been engaging the farm's defenders since 0710hrs (ten minutes after Group II had set off), and had steadily pushed into the rows of cultivated trees to its east. As the only A7V in the area, 541 received considerable, but ineffectual, small-arms and machine-gun fire as it roamed through the sector. Block's mount nearly 'bellied' on top of the surrounding wall, but the vehicle's weight and momentum soon crushed the obstruction, and dispersed the men of 2nd West Yorkshire in the immediate area. After two hours of fighting, the tank helped eliminate resistance alongside the advancing 93rd Reserve Infantry Regiment, and emerged at the farm's western perimeter. To the south, A7Vs 562 and 'Gretchen' (501) achieved similar success. After helping to repulse an enemy counter-attack, the trio continued on toward the next objective, the sparse, lofty trees of the Bois d'Aquenne. Lappe, however, became disoriented in the thinning fog, and manoeuvred 'Gretchen' to within 30m of British infantry, who responded with close-range rifle and machine-gun fire directed against the vehicle's various openings. Wounded, the driver stalled 'Gretchen', and with brakes sticking and gears tight, the crew dismounted to fight as infantry. After a brief pause in which to let the engines cool, Lappe withdrew with what crewmen could be gathered in the confusion, and set off again.

## THE FIRST TANK BATTLE

Amid a heavy German artillery bombardment between the Bois l'Abbé and the oncoming 5th Guards Foot Regiment and 93rd Reserve Infantry Regiment, Mitchell negotiated his Mark IV toward the Cachy Switch. His crew continued to struggle with swollen eyes and inflamed skin resulting from the morning's gas attack, as much of the residue lingered inside the enclosed tank. To his right, 1st Section's crews in the two accompanying females under Lieutenants Edward Hawthorne and J. Webber suffered similarly as the trio skirted the Bois d'Aquenne and entered the fray. As Mitchell approached the discontinuous, hastily dug line of trenches between Cachy and Villers-Bretonneux, his concern about the apparent lack of supporting infantry was suddenly answered when an excited British soldier climbed up to ground level to report that enemy tanks were about. Invigorated at the opportunity to engage his German equivalent, Mitchell opened a loophole to see the *Feldgrau*-coloured 'Nixe' (561) approaching half a kilometre away from the south-east, its front marked with a pair of chalky white Roman 'V' numerals indicating it was ATD 2's fifth vehicle. As neither Mitchell nor most of his fellow tankers had been briefed on what enemy armour looked like, let alone its capabilities, British propaganda's touting of the near invincibility of their own tanks undoubtedly weighed on his mind as he sized up the tracked blockhouse as it lumbered across the rough farmland. Following close behind, waves of 5th Guards Grenadier and 419th Reserve Infantry Regiments swarmed over the crest, running toward the south-eastern horizon.

As Mitchell's tank continued to traverse the friendly trenches carefully, so as to not crush their occupants, the Mark IV's gunners crouched expectantly beside their loaded 6-pounder cannon. Apparently unseen by the oncoming German vehicle, as 4086 approached a small section of barbed wire, the starboard gunner, Sgt J.R. McKenzie, fired a sighting shot at the armoured target, which burst well behind 'Nixe' (561). A follow-up round landed just to the right, but neither prompted a response. Before a third round could be fired, 5th Guards Grenadier Regiment treated the Mark IV to a machine-gun broadside that lit up the dark interior with numerous stinging sparks and flying metal splinters. Most of the crew had dropped to the relative safety of the deck, so the driver drove straight ahead amid a second machine-gun burst.

With fog lifting, Biltz could see Cachy off to the west as he moved toward the Bois d'Aquenne. Partially obscured by the dark treeline and artillery smoke, he suddenly sighted Brown's Mark IVs and ordered 'Nixe' (561) to reverse to a better position from which to engage. Behind the German tank, assault infantry continued to advance as they, and their British contemporaries, watched the unfolding drama of history's first tank-on-tank engagement. Unable to counter their armoured adversary effectively, the machine-gun-armed British females were at a considerable disadvantage, especially as the A7V's rudimentary suspension and superior speed imparted greater manoeuvrability to Biltz, even though both were hampered by the rough terrain. Biltz stopped to fire his 57mm cannon at Mitchell; inside a distance of 1,000m the flat-bottomed rounds used by both sides produced eddies and wobbling that interfered with accurate trajectories at such close ranges. Believing he had knocked out the male, Biltz turned his attention to the two females, and quickly holed them, leaving sizeable openings in each hull which exposed their crews to German small-arms and machine-gun fire.

View encompassing the Bois d'Aquenne, where Mitchell encountered Biltz. Between the road's crest and Villers-Bretonneux, Uihlein's ATD 3 moved up to the Bois d'Aquenne. (Author)

Unscathed, Mitchell took advantage of a dip in the ground, to reposition his Mark IV (4086) to better target 'Nixe' using the port sponson. Hampered by a swollen right eye, an absent loader and a suspensionless vehicle that bounced excessively over the rough terrain, the gunner's first shot landed some 30m in front of the A7V, and a second sailed past, as Biltz continued toward the Bois d'Aquenne in the mistaken belief that the immediate British tank threat had been eliminated. Amid the falling artillery rounds, Mitchell watched with astonishment as the badly damaged females limped to the rear, when another round of machine-gun fire struck his vehicle, and seriously wounded one of the Lewis gunners in both legs. To improve the chances of hitting the target, Mitchell advanced at a slower pace, but it offered scant improvement as the port gunner, registering carefully, hit the ground right in front of the A7V. Mitchell moved the tank to reposition McKenzie for another try, this time from a stopped, stable vehicle platform, but the gunner continued to miss the target.

The pause was eventually justified as it allowed McKenzie to carefully lay his No. 4 Mk III sighting scope, which resulted in him finally striking 'Nixe' on its starboard front plate just beside the main gun. The impact killed the 57mm gun operator, mortally wounded two crewmen, and slightly wounded three others. Two more rounds struck its starboard flank, which damaged an oil mechanism, and forced the vehicle to a stop lest additional movement disable it. As 'Nixe' carried ammunition, a box of hand grenades, and other potentially explosive materiel, the crew abandoned the tank, fearing additional hits on the hull. Mitchell responded by ordering his machine-gunners to target the German tankers as they dispersed, but with 'Siegfried' (525) and 'Schnuck' (504) spotted en route toward Cachy he broke contact, and focused on the new threat. Once the A7V's engines had cooled, and were found to be functioning, the crew remounted, and coaxed the stricken 'Nixe' some 2km to the rear before the loss of oil finally immobilized it. The vehicle was salvaged later that evening.

A view showing where, along the southern horizon, Müller and Bitter turned away from Cachy. (Author)

By 1100hrs Villers-Bretonneux was under German control, with 207th Reserve Infantry Regiment along the town's western outskirts, while the division's reserve, 35th Fusilier Regiment, moved up behind it. As the clearing smoke and fog promoted an increase in British artillery fire, and with his primary objective secured, Skopnik withdrew with the rest of Group I to their starting point at the Marcelcave sugar factory. At the opposite end of Villers-Bretonneux, Leutnant Bürmann's 'Cyklop' (507) and Leutnant Hennecke's 'Baden I' (505), each with *Bocklafetten* cannon, and camouflaged with small clay-yellow and reddish-brown blotches, skirted the railway station and assisted German infantry, who were crossing the Cachy Switch, and entering the Bois d'Aquenne.

## ENTER THE WHIPPETS

Having spotted the German 257th Reserve and 419th Infantry Regiments within 400m of Cachy, in what looked like a staging area for an attack against the village, an Allied reconnaissance plane dropped a message to alert 58th (2/1st London) Division to the threat. In response, as part of the effort to stem the German advance at the Cachy Switch, at 1030hrs 'X' Company's seven Whippets were ordered to move up from their positions at the Bois de Blangy, just west of the Bois l'Abbé. Formed from the Tank Corps' 'C' Company, 3rd Battalion, as an emergency formation for the defence of Amiens, it was on the scene within the hour, and preparing to pre-empt the anticipated German attack. To ascertain the terrain over which his command would soon fight, Acting Captain Tommy Price rode ahead on horseback, meeting Captain Sheppard from 2nd Northamptonshire, who briefed him on the immediate situation.

By 1140hrs, Bürmann had manoeuvred his pale green and *Feldgrau*-painted vehicle as far as the Roman road west of Villers-Bretonneux, where he came under fire from a British field gun detailed to cover the intersection. Although the first round missed, the second struck the A7V, and as Bürmann attempted to withdraw, a third exploded under the vehicle's rear, but besides the concussion on the hull the percussion shrapnel did little damage. Hennecke's 'Baden I' (505) covered Bürmann's southern flank, although with a damaged 57mm cannon, Hennecke's response was limited. As Block and Bartens were operating just to the south, the four A7Vs provided support for 93rd Reserve Infantry Regiment and 5th Guards Grenadier Regiment as they crossed the Cachy Switch and entered the Bois d'Aquenne. Around noon, 1st Sherwood Foresters unsuccessfully counter-attacked toward Villers-Bretonneux from the west, but Bürmann and Hennecke helped fight them off. 2nd Royal Berkshires attempted a similar operation near Hill 104, but were forced to withdraw to the north.

Instead of remaining with Hennecke and Bürmann as the pair advanced toward the gap between Villers-Bretonneux and the Bois d'Aquenne, Leutnant Heinz Theunissen directed 'Mephisto' (506) against what resistance remained around Monument Farm, and help secure 5th Guards Grenadier Regiment's area of operations. The third of three *Bocklafette* A7Vs, 'Mephisto' sported an emblem of a red devil spiriting away a British tank over a reddish-brown and *Feldgrau* camouflage scheme, which made it rather more distinctive than its brethren. Having already captured some 250 prisoners earlier in the day, Theunissen found as he approached the compound that the fuel hoses had clogged, which forced him to stop briefly for repairs. On resuming his drive west of the farm, Theunissen's tank became inextricably stuck in one of the area's large

**OVERLEAF:**
Following the 'holing' of two Mark IV (female) tanks by 'Nixe', which forced the British tanks to withdraw from the Cachy Switch, 2nd Lieutenant Frank Mitchell's Mark IV (male) engages his German adversary, striking its starboard plate.

A captured Mark A Whippet, with an Iron Cross, undergoing testing at BAKP 20's proving ground at Monceau-sur-Sambre (western Charleroi, Belgium), minus its .303in Hotchkiss machine guns. The vehicle's agility is evident, but none was reused in combat by the Germans. (NARA)

shell holes, and like 'Elfriede' (542) became another victim of the A7V design's vision-blocking extended front and rear. That night, a German engineer officer was sent out to destroy the latter, some 600m west of 'Mephisto' (506). Unaware that two disabled A7Vs were in proximity he mistakenly damaged Theunissen's stricken vehicle, which remained in no-man's land until 26th Battalion AIF recovered it on 14 July 1918.

At around 1220hrs, 'X' Company initiated its attack from the Cachy Switch, with roughly 40m between the advancing Whippets. The startled Germans, many of whom were eating a midday meal, scrambled to meet the new threat. Within ten minutes, the machine-gun-armed vehicles were upon them, but without an effective anti-tank counter immediately available, and caught in generally open terrain, the defenders quickly tried to disengage. With 'Schnuck' (504) further to the south, Bitter saw forward elements of 332nd and 419th Infantry Regiments withdrawing on an extended front from the Cachy sector. Quickly making contact with I./IR332's commander, who asked for help in stabilizing the situation, the tank commander manoeuvred his *Feldgrau*-coloured 'Siegfried' (525) to engage the rampaging British medium tanks.

To protect 4th Guards Infantry Division's weakened left flank, 2nd Battery, 6th Guards Field Artillery Regiment provided 77mm support from the ridge near the Bois d'Hangard. Although these rounds landed among the Whippets, it appeared Bitter was able to hit 2nd Lieutenant Harry Dale's Whippet (A256) at 200m with his second 57mm shot, which set the British tank on fire. Bitter then turned to address 2nd Lt D.M. Roberts's (A255) at 700m, and repeated the process, again finding success with his second round. Damaged beyond repair, both Whippets were later scrapped. 'Siegfried' could not help, as the striker spring on the firing pin had broken under stress, so Bitter resorted to using his remaining two machine guns on 2nd Lieutenant George Richie's (A244), which soon immobilized and ignited it. Those British tankers who survived would have expected no quarter, having killed and wounded so many Germans; also, during 1917 many British tankers had been summarily killed after being captured.

With almost half of their number gone, the remaining four Whippets turned back, and in the process repeated their swathe of destruction through the German infantrymen. Müller's 'Schnuck' (504), having been delayed by fog, finally arrived to hit 'Crawick' (A236) under 2nd Lieutenant Thomas Oldham, which was withdrawing. Although immobilized and on fire, A244 and A236 were later recovered by No. 2 Salvage Company, refurbished and eventually returned to operational status. 'Crossmichael' (A233), 'Centaur III' (A277) and 'Crustacean III' (A286) returned to British lines at around 1530hrs, and remained available for further action. Having been exposed to heavy artillery fire in the flat, open terrain east of Cachy, machine-gun fire from the village, and partially overrun by the British Whippets, 77th Reserve Division's infantrymen made a final half-hearted advance before digging trenches roughly 1,000m to the east of their Cachy objective.

At 1300hrs Grove's two-tank section from 'A' Company, 1st Battalion, went into action near Bürmann's vacated position, and dispersed what German infantry were probing the area. While Lieutenant Charles Gibbons' male remained in place to provide support from the west side of the railway, 2nd Lieutenant S.C. Bell's female crossed the tracks north of the Roman road, and entered the outskirts of Villers-Bretonneux, where the British tank came under heavy enemy machine-gun fire from several of the buildings. Within half an hour, 39th Field

Looking east from along the Cachy Switch (the D168) crest toward Villers-Bretonneux. The Amiens–Tergnier railway runs just this side of the light-coloured buildings on the left and right, with the steeple of St John the Baptist's church in the centre background. Destroyed in April 1918, the neo-Romanesque/ Byzantine-style church was rebuilt in 1929. (Author)

Artillery Regiment, 228th Infantry Division, immobilized the male with 77mm fire. With four of Bell's machine guns knocked out, three crewmen wounded, and 1st Worcestershire requesting that the Whippet withdraw as it was drawing too much German fire, he withdrew from the fight.

With 'Nixe' (561) out of the fight, Mitchell moved toward Cachy to close the range with 'Schnuck' (504) and 'Siegfried' (525), but accurate targeting was again hampered by the constant bumping and swaying that resulted from crossing shell holes and irregular farmland. As precision was not as important when attacking large infantry formations, in the interim, Mitchell directed 6-pounder canister into the nearby 419th Infantry Regiment. As the A7Vs approached their objective, the British 58th Battalion, Machine Gun Corps, subjected 'Schnuck' (504) to heavy machine-gun fire. Division-assigned to trouble spots, the unit's authorized 64 Vickers machine guns (nearly double the number of machine guns assigned to an infantry battalion) proved an effective deterrent to further German infantry efforts before Cachy. As Mitchell got within effective range, he ordered a few sighting shells fired at 'Siegfried' (525), which, like its partner, had done what it could to help 77th Reserve Division capture the plateau west of Villers-Bretonneux, and which then withdrew toward German lines at around 1545hrs.

As it was the only British asset above ground, German artillery focused on Mitchell's Mark IV, which tried to vacate the area. En route to the relative safety behind British positions along the Cachy Switch, 4086 zigzagged to hamper determined, German artillery shelling aimed directly at it. A German aircraft added to the effort as it flew in at some 30m (just over the field guns' trajectories), and dropped a bomb directly in front of the jouking tank, which thrust its front violently skyward; undamaged, 4086 continued on. Watching the unfolding drama, a light-mortar section from 5th Guards Grenadier Regiment lobbed three rounds near the vehicle, which apparently helped them acquire the range, as a fourth destroyed two track plates, and forced the remaining segments into a bunched-up cluster. With his vehicle circling uncontrollably, Mitchell ordered 4086 stopped, and the remaining 6-pounder rounds fired at targets along the crest halfway to Villers-Bretonneux. Once ammunition was exhausted, and with no further combat options, the crew abandoned the vehicle and scrambled to the relative safety of a nearby trench.

British infantry prepare to retake Villers-Bretonneux during the night of 23/24 April 1918. (H.D. Girdwood)

## AUSTRALIAN COUNTER-ATTACK

Even though the German offensive had been anticipated for several days, the speed of the operation was such that the British III Corps commander, Butler, had not even realized Villers-Bretonneux and Bois d'Aquenne had been attacked until after they were overrun. His emphasis on spit and polish did little to compensate for poor planning and combat training, resulting in the Germans taking over 2,400 prisoners during the engagement, and leaving the British in a seemingly precarious position. With fresh Dominion units idling on the flanks as a reserve, however, the British decided to use them as a counter-attacking force to regain the territory lost earlier in the day.

As part of a two-pronged operation to pinch off Villers-Bretonneux, Brigadier General William Glasgow's largely green 13th Australian Infantry Brigade set off toward Monument Farm at 2200hrs, with no preliminary bombardment. At a quarter to midnight, Brigadier General H.E. 'Pompey' Elliot's 15th Australian Infantry Brigade followed suit, and as the German 243rd Infantry Division had failed to take Hill 104, the Australian unit achieved considerable success in swinging north of the town as far as the abandoned aerodrome. The southern prong, however, was unable to close the developing perimeter. Although the Australians demonstrated considerable dash and aggression, frequently in compliance with orders to take no prisoners, they did not clear the Bois d'Aquenne and enter the town until dawn. German progress towards Amiens had reached its zenith, and on 27 April the Australians finally recaptured Villers-Bretonneux.

# STATISTICS AND ANALYSIS

Although the Germans had early on considered the development of an armoured/tracked/technical solution to help break the operational stalemate of the Western Front, limited supplies of men and materiel meant they were unable, or unwilling, to invest the necessary resources and effort towards creating a large armoured force and supporting infrastructure. Many conservative senior commanders believed tanks to be little more than a proof of concept or unnecessary diversion, and agreed with Ludendorff's assessment that 'The best arms against the tanks are the nerves, discipline, and intrepidity.' Interdepartmental squabbling between the War Office and OHL also persisted to the detriment of what limited potential the German tank programme had. By the time the dramatic, albeit temporary, success of massed British tanks at Cambrai in November 1917 had demonstrated the success of the concept, it was too late to rectify existing manufacturing and logistical deficiencies effectively, or redistribute resources from more proven elements such as specialist *Stosstruppen*. While these represented an excellent tactical solution to overcome a specific battlefield problem, the lack of mechanization severely limited logistics, and consequently endurance. Reciprocally, a defence in depth backed by purpose-built anti-tank weapons, mines, direct-firing artillery, mortars and ground-attack *Schlachtflieger* units committed en masse at decisive locations seemed an effective solution to countering Allied infantry and armour assaults.

When the first German tank manual came out in January 1918, the tank was presented as an auxiliary weapon that could overrun barbed-wire and gun emplacements, and potentially deposit a contingent of assault infantry, but not decide a battle on

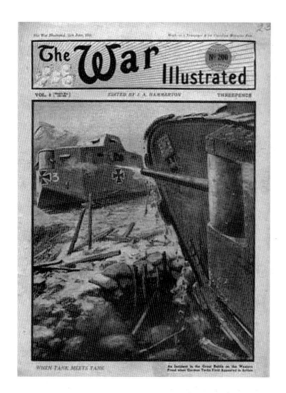

The War Illustrated magazine's stylized cover illustration of the first-ever tank battle at Villers-Bretonneux. (The War Illustrated)

its own. The manual further stated that 'The infantry and tanks will advance independently of one another', and that 'No special instructions regarding the cooperation with tanks will be issued'. While assault infantry had practised and improved upon their trade, both they and the A7V crews struggled to coordinate assets to best achieve a battlefield solution. In contrast, British War Office publications stressed the role of the tank not just in supporting infantry, but in integrating with it to obtain an objective. Very like the trial and error of designing, producing and sustaining armoured vehicles in the field, the establishment of a training programme to implement new, often novel theories proved difficult, as there was scant precedent upon which to rely.

In combat the A7V was well-suited for its intended role, owing to its front-mounted main gun, which when engaging a target correspondingly presented its thickest armour and smallest profile for any return fire. Its side and rear armour was adequate for most operations against infantry, but the roof louvres, flaps and openings were vulnerable to shrapnel and machine-gun fire. Similar in weight and size to its Mark IV (male) contemporary, the German tank possessed, at least on paper, twice the maximum speed over level surfaces, owing in part perhaps to its greatest asset, sprung bogies. The A7V also possessed twice as many machine guns as its rival, and could produce a withering fire over nearly 360 degrees, while its Quick Firing 57mm cannon proved useful when attacking both soft targets, using high-explosive and canister shot, and hard targets, using *panzerkopf* shells.

The German tank was handicapped by a variety of problems. Its unmodified Holt tractor configuration resulted in a front idler that was too small and low, which in combination with a low front hindered cross-country movement. An over-large gearbox reduced ground clearance, engines were prone to overheating as there was no airflow to cool the radiator, the cooling system was overtaxed, and the weak frame could become distorted under a load without being strengthened. Mechanical breakdowns were common, and a shortage of spare parts necessitated having two mechanics on board. A7V crew cohesion was hampered as they came from different services and backgrounds, and comfort and ergonomics were a low design priority. The A7V's bulky shape made for numerous blind spots, especially for the driver, and made the vehicle an excellent target. Command and control within the A7V was difficult, as except for a commander/gunner signal-light arrangement, orders to other parts of the tank required a crewman to move about to convey them. The periscope for aiming was small, and the field of vision wavered during the tank's movement, which made accurate target-finding impossible except when the vehicle was stationary.

In a combat environment with very few tank-on-tank engagements (they occurred just twice during the war, at Villers-Bretonneux on 24 April 1918 (A7V vs Mark IV/ Whippet) and Mark IV vs Mark IV (*Beute*) at Niergnies/Séranvillers on 8 October 1918)

– the A7V held its own under reasonable battlefield conditions. As only 20 were produced, numbers simply did not exist to maintain momentum while suffering battlefield and mechanical attrition. Once the Germans moved to the operational defensive in mid-1918, A7Vs lost on the battlefield could not easily be recovered – a problem that also eliminated capturing foreign models for reuse. Ultimately the German tank programme was an ad hoc effort. Although the product could achieve local successes under optimum environmental and support conditions – due mostly to a lack of Allied anti-tank capabilities – the extremely limited numbers of German tanks meant they could not affect the larger operation.

As with artillery, machine guns and mortars, British Mark IVs were to be used primarily to support the infantry in gaining superiority of fire, and to provide a degree of mutual protection. The accompanying soldiers both provided the eyes and ears for the buttoned-up crews and secured captured ground. To address this role most effectively, the British opted for producing more numerous, less heavily armed and armoured vehicles, as opposed to limited numbers of heavy tanks. As the Mark IV was resistant to rifle fire, shrapnel, and to a lesser degree machine-gun and armour-piercing rounds, it offered an adequate amount of protection for those inside, and outside. When used in sufficient numbers to keep a defender from focusing on a limited number of vehicles, those on the receiving end contended with the psychological effects of being overwhelmed, with little recourse save withdrawing.

By early 1918, British tanks had participated in combat for 18 months, and although the first year was fraught with mismanagement and inexperience, persistence and mass production were finally paying battlefield dividends. Hard-learned combat lessons were steadily incorporated into an effective practice, which broadened to include a host of new vehicle types and applications. Perhaps most importantly, British commanders were seeing the benefit of massing tanks to support attacks against key battlefield locations. With such high attrition rates among tanks of the era, large numbers of available vehicles provided parts for disabled vehicles, and a reserve to exploit tactically or to counter unforeseen battlefield situations. Effective standardized training reflected the importance British authorities placed in the concept, although tactical employment was often suspect. The Mark IV's pair of side-mounted 6-pounder guns offered twice the available firepower of the A7V, and presented a reduced vehicle silhouette, but their use greatly stretched manufacturing efforts to produce the cannon. Engaging targets also necessitated offering much of the tank's side – a dangerous endeavour when confronting Germany's very effective 77mm field cannon.

Although a major contribution to the Allies' battlefield success in mid- and late 1918, and even though British tank authorities conservatively estimated that one Allied tank had the combat equivalent of some 500 infantrymen, the Mark IV (and tanks in general) did not provide a war-winning element in isolation. By the time tracked armoured vehicles were available in significant numbers to participate effectively in mobile operations, they were often worn out, damaged, or destroyed in such numbers that they could not usefully exploit late-war German operational withdrawals, and penetrate the enemy's rear areas. Tanks were also unable to operate in swampy, heavily wooded or shelled terrain. Visibility from inside a tank was restricted, necessitating objectives to be easily recognisable via direct routes. Allied tanks did, however, make static defences vulnerable to tactical penetration and flanking, and forced a battlefield tempo upon the

Marker along the Cachy Switch (the D168) stating in German, French and English: 'Here on the 24th of April 1918, the first ever tank battle took place between German and British armour.' (Author)

defending Germans that could not be effectively countered, especially when they were used in concert with accurate heavy artillery fire and aircraft. By 1918, the British and French had produced some 2,636 and 3,900 tanks respectively, and were planning to build many more the following year. The Germans were outproduced by roughly 320:1, and their combat deployment of 30 Mark IV (*Beute*) tanks (out of 78 captured) amounted to little more than an experiment.

As the size and scope of the Tank Corps grew, questions were raised as to expanding existing theory, as lighter, faster tanks, such as the Mark A Whippet and Renault FT, appeared to have the potential for achieving deep-penetrating, indirect battles, and avoiding costly direct actions aimed at physically defeating an enemy force. One such solution, forwarded by J.F.C. Fuller as 'Plan 1919', heralded the use of independent tank formations, which, accompanied by aerial support, would penetrate an enemy's defences, range against their command, control and logistics assets, and disrupt efforts to organize and commit reinforcements. Although the concept of employing speed, mobility and firepower to produce shock and decisive victory originated during the war, by its end the British lacked such a vehicle; nor did they have the resources and inclination to create it. Such ideas were left to be fleshed out during the 1920s and '30s by such theorists as Germany's Heinz Guderian and the Soviet Union's Mikhail Tukhachevsky.

| Tank Attrition | | | | | |
|---|---|---|---|---|---|
| Location | Date | Committed | Ditched/ broken down | Immobilized/ destroyed | % lost* |
| Flers-Courcelette (Br) | 15 Sep 16 | 49 | 31 | 9 | 82 |
| Bullecourt (Br) | 11 Apr 17 | 12 | 1 | 8 | 75 |
| Berry-au-Bac (Fr) | 16 Apr 17 | 121 | 15 | 66 | 67 |
| Messines (Br) | 7 Jun 17 | 72 | 48 | 11 | 82 |
| Passchendaele (Br) | 31 Jul 17 | 136 | 42 combined + 75 bogged down | | 86 |
| Cambrai (Br) | 20 Nov 17 | 350 | 114 | 65 | 51 |
| Saint-Quentin (Gr) | 21 Mar 18 | 5 + 5 *Beute* | 3 | 2 | 50 |
| Villers-Bretonneux (Br/Gr) | 24 Apr 18 | 12/13 | 0/2 | 6/1 | 50/23 |
| Matz Valley (Fr) | 11 Jun 18 | 144 | 63 combined | | 44 |
| Hamel (Br) | 4 Jul 18 | 60 | 3 | 0 | 5 |
| Soissons (Fr) | 18 Jul 18 | 346 | 121 | 102 | 64 |
| Amiens (Br) | 8 Aug 18 | 414 | 269 combined | | 65 |
| Niergnies/Séranvillers (Br/Gr) | 8 Oct 18 | 8/8 *Beute* | 1/4 | 1/2 | 25/75 |
| *Many vehicles 'lost' on the respective day's attack were later recovered to be cannibalized, converted or refurbished. | | | | | |

# AFTERMATH

As Operation *Michael* had spluttered to a stop when the Germans expended their strength and exceeded their logistic capability, the Amiens sector had correspondingly drawn British forces in at the expense of other fronts. Having anticipated such a scenario, Ludendorff unleashed peripheral offences to the north at Lys (9–29 April), and the south at Aisne (27 May–4 June), Noyon–Montdidier (8–12 June) and Champagne–Marne (15–17 July), in an attempt to maintain momentum and keep

During the battle, 2nd West Yorkshire's headquarters was near the Villers-Bretonneux railway station. (L. Caron)

the Allied forces off-balance and reactive. While these operations were tactical successes, in that they had ruptured Allies lines on a broad front for the first time in over three years, Ludendorff's Peace Offensive failed to cripple enemy efforts in northern France quickly, and force a favourable armistice. By the end of July 1918, Germany was exhausted in the field as well as at home.

Forced back into a defensive posture yet again, senior German commanders anticipated Allied counter-offensives against the Saint-Mihiel front east of Reims, or in Flanders near Lille or Ypres.

2. - VILLERS-BRETONNEUX (Somme). — Vue générale de la Gare.

Introduced in mid-June 1918, the Renault FT's top-mounted, single rotating turret and three-man crew profoundly influenced subsequent tank designs. (Author)

The Allies had already mounted several local counter-offensives in these areas to gain immediate objectives to improve their defensive positions, as well as distract attention from the centre east of Amiens. Their forces were growing in strength, as more American units arrived in France, and British reinforcements were transferred from the Sinai and Palestine as those campaigns wound down. The successful use of French tanks at Soissons, and the surprising British victory at Hamel on 4 July 1918 convinced many who had remained sceptical of the tank concept to now call for greater production numbers.

When the British counter-attack was launched east of Amiens on 8 August 1918, it heralded what was later known as the Hundred Days Offensive – a series of engagements that ultimately forced an end to the war. The British Fourth Army's rapid, armour-incorporating thrust could not be effectively countered, which resulted in morale rising commensurately with the number of German prisoners taken. In contrast, the British Third Army, with no armoured support, had almost no effect on the line. With the front ruptured, the Allies steadily forced the Germans back to the Hindenburg Line, and beyond. Foch's corresponding Grand Offensive focused numerous attacks designed to sever German lateral communications, and progressively gain ground along a wide front.

As the Kaiser's beleaguered army withdrew from territory it had held for over three years large amounts of heavy equipment and supplies were abandoned. This reduced the Germans' morale and capacity to resist. Allied commanders and political leaders optimistically believed that victory could be achieved by the year's end, and negated the anticipated buildup for a decisive effort in 1919. The German sailors' revolt during the night of 29/30 October 1918 at Wilhelmshaven spread across the nation within days. It led to the proclamation of a republic on 9 November 1918, and Kaiser Wilhelm II's abdication. An armistice was signed two days later (ratified on 10 January 1920), which ushered in the draconian terms of the Versailles Treaty, which attempted to bankrupt and humiliate Germany – a festering wound that would motivate many to seek retribution, and bring about another world war within two decades. When Reichstag officials confronted the German High Command in October 1918, demanding an explanation for its sudden decision to sue for peace, the latter stated that 'Two factors have had a decisive influence on our decision, namely, tanks and our reserves', and that 'Solely owing to the success of the tanks, we have suffered enormous losses in prisoners'.

# BIBLIOGRAPHY

## PRIMARY SOURCES

### BUNDESARCHIV-MILITÄRARCHIV, FREIBURG

RH 61/50770: Gr. Hauptquartier an KM (A7V) vom 2.3.1918/Chef d. Genst. d. Feldheeres Iv Nr. 50257 op. vom 15.3.1917. Zur Beurteilung des A7V durch die OHL.

PH 3/355: Anleitung für die Verwendung von Sturm-Panzerkraftwagen-Abteilung, 18 January 1918.

### PUBLIC RECORDS OFFICE, KEW

95/82 Controller of Salvage (July 1917–January 1919)

95/93 Headquarters Tank Corps (January–May 1918)

95/105 3 Brigade Tank Corps (January 1918–January 1919)

95/106 3 Brigade Tank Corps: 3 Battalion (April 1917–March 1919)

95/109 4 Brigade Tank Corps: 1 Battalion (May 1917–March 1919)

95/117 Central Tank Workshops (January 1917–October 1919)

297/2560 Villers-Bretonneux (24/25 April 1918)

# SECONDARY SOURCES

Balck, William, *Entwicklung der Taktik im Weltkriege*, R. Eisenschmidt, Berlin (1922)

Bean, Charles Edwin Woodrow, *The Australian Imperial Force in France during the German Offensive, 1918*, University of Queensland Press, Brisbane (1983)

Biltz, Friedrich Wilhelm, 'Bericht über das erste Gefecht einer Panzerwagens gegen englische Tanks', *Die Kraftfahrkampftruppe* 4, pp 1–8, (1937)

Brown, Ian Malcolm, *British Logistics on the Western Front: 1914–1919*, Greenwood, Westport, CT (1998)

Browne, Douglas Gordon, *The Tank in Action*, William Blackwood and Sons, Edinburgh and London (1920)

Edmonds, Sir James Edward, *Military Operations, France and Belgium, 1918*, The Battery Press, Nashville, TN (1995)

Fuller, J.F.C., *Tanks in the Great War, 1914–1918*, E.P. Dutton & Co., Boston, MA (1920)

Fuller, J.F.C., *The Reformation of War*, Hutchinson, London (1923)

Fuller, J.F.C., *The Foundations of the Science of War*, Hutchinson, London (1925)

Gruss, Hellmuth, *Die Deutschen Sturmbataillone Im Weltkrieg*, Junker & Dünnhaupt, Berlin (1938)

Hickey, Daniel Edgar, *Rolling into Action: Memoirs of a Tank Corps Section Commander*, Naval & Military Press Ltd, Uckfield (2007)

Hundleby, Maxwell & Strasheim, Rainer, *The German A7V Tank and the Captured British Mark IV Tanks of World War I*, Haynes Publications, Yeovil (1990)

Hundleby, Maxwell & Strasheim, Rainer, *Sturmpanzer A7V: First of the Panzers*, Tankograd Publishing, Erlangen (2010)

A dramatic example of the damage caused by artillery. The centre soldier sports an Iron Cross 2nd Class (ribbon in second button hole), while his comrade wears a marksman lanyard (one acorn) and a Pertrix 669 *Taschenlampe* ('pocket light'). (NARA)

Lane, Michael R., *The Story of the Wellington Foundry, Lincoln: History of William Foster & Co. Ltd*, Unicorn Press, London (1997)

Ludendorff, Erich, *Meine Kriegserinnerungen 1914–1918*, E.S. Mittler & Sohn, Berlin (1919)

Mitchell, Frank, *Tank Warfare: The Story of the Tanks in the Great War*, Naval and Military Press Ltd, Uckfield (2009)

Petter, Erich, *Kampfwagen-Abwehr im Weltkriege 1914–1918*, Chef der Heeresleitung, (1932)

Petter, Erich, *Die technische Entwicklung der deutschen Kampfwagen im Weltkrieges 1914–1918*, Chef der Heeresleitung, (1932)

Rohrbeck, Karl-August, *Taktik. Ein Handbuch auf Grund der Erfahrungen im Weltkrieges*, Mittler & Sohn, Berlin (1919)

Schaible, Ulla, *Sturmpanzerwagen A7V*, Bernard & Graefe Verlag, Bonn (2003)

Volckheim, Ernst von, *Der Kampfwagen in der heutigen Kriegführung*, E.S. Mittler & Sohn, Berlin (1924)

Volckheim, Ernst von, *Betrachtungen über Kampfwagen-Organisation und Verwendung*, E.S. Mittler & Sohn, Berlin (1924)

Volckheim, Ernst von, *Kampfwagen und Abwehr dagegen*, E.S. Mittler & Sohn, Berlin (1925)

Volckheim, Ernst von, *Deutsche Kampfwagen greifen an!*, E.S. Mittler & Sohn, Berlin (1937)

Volckheim, Ernst von, *Die Deutschen Kampfwagen im Weltkrieg*, Unitall Verlag, Radolfzell (2008)

Watson, William Henry Lowe, *A Company of Tanks*, William Blackwood and Sons, Edinburgh and London (1920)

Whitmore, Mark, *Mephisto – A7V Sturmpanzerwagen 506 – a History of the Sole Surviving First World War German Tank*, Queensland Museum, Brisbane (1989)

Williams-Ellis, Clough & Williams-Ellis, Amabel, *The Tank Corps*, G.H. Doran, New York, NY (1919)

Wilson, George Murray, *Fighting Tanks: An Account of the Royal Tank Corps in Action, 1916–1919*, Seeley, Service & Co. Ltd, London (1929)

Zabecki, David T., *The German 1918 Offensives: A Case Study in the Operational Level of War*, Psychology Press, London (2006)

# INDEX